The Future Metropolis

The Future Metropolis

Edited by

LLOYD RODWIN

George Braziller
NEW YORK

All rights in this book are reserved.
For information, address the publisher:

George Braziller, Inc.

One Park Avenue

New York 10016

Library of Congress Catalog Card Number: 61-9964

Printed in the United States of America

Prefatory Note

In draft form, the essays in this book were discussed in a closed conference—jointly planned and sponsored by the Tamiment Institute and DÆDALUS, the Journal of the American Academy of Arts and Sciences—that met at Tamiment-in-the-Poconos in the Spring of 1960. The essays appeared subsequently in the Winter 1961 issue of DÆDALUS, for which Kevin Lynch and I served as guest editors.

Special thanks are due our gracious hosts, Mr. Ben Josephson, the Director of Tamiment-in-the-Poconos, and Dr. Norman Jacobs, the Educational Director of Tamiment. I am also indebted to the Editors of DÆDALUS, who provided many helpful suggestions.

Kevin Lynch worked with me on every phase of this effort and he deserves a major share of whatever credit may be associated with this volume. This opportunity to collaborate with Professor Lynch, as on other occasions, was a richly satisfying experience.

—LLOYD RODWIN

Contents

1. A World of Cities

KEVIN LYNCH and LLOYD RODWIN

ALTHOUGH THE CITY itself is five thousand years old, the metropolis is a new phenomenon, dating from a mere hundred years ago. Its scale alone differentiates it from any older type of urban settlement. Even ancient Rome, with its million inhabitants, was in visible relation to its surrounding countryside. One could easily walk from one district to another or from the central to the rural area. In the metropolis this is hardly possible; even in a car it may take hours to move from center to periphery. Thus the city has swollen to a vast organism whose scale far transcends individual control.

Throughout the metropolis the environment is man-made— even its plants and trees are there by man's agency. Yet the density of its population in the outer parts, at least, is much lower than in the traditional city, so that we observe single dwellings and factories dispersed among gardens, parks, small woods, and open spaces. In the suburb, city and country fuse, and their long rivalry may here find its resolution.

It appears that these metropolitan complexes will become the dominant environment, at least in the most highly developed regions of the world, for they contain the bulk of the population, and they produce and consume most of the goods. The living space will become a set of such areas, at times separated by areas of low population that provide raw materials. The metropolitan regions may be very large, even grouped in chains several hundred miles long; but they will be more or less continuously urbanized, however low their suburban densities may be. Each one will display a continuous dense web of facilities for communication, within which the population will be highly interdependent on a daily basis in terms of supply, of information, and of commutation to and from work. Such a society will be intricate and its means of communication will be increasingly mechanized and depersonalized. Most likely it will also be mobile and egalitarian. This type of mass habitation and this kind of inhabitant may well become a world-wide pattern.

These are some of the prospects that prompted *Dædalus,* the Journal of the American Academy of Arts and Sciences, to devote an issue to the challenge of the metropolis. As guest editors of this issue, which was the genesis of the present book, we charged the contributors with the task of examining how metropolitan development could be controlled so as to ease the transitional phases and avoid disastrous consequences. We suggested that they assume that, in significant areas of the world and within a period as short as fifty years, the majority of the world's population will be accommodated in vast metropolitan complexes, each on a scale of twenty million people or more. Staggering as this figure may seem, it is by no means unreasonable, and even if exaggerated, it sets the stage for an evaluation of this new phenomenon in the history of society. We asked them to consider what might be lost in such a future world, and even more importantly, to define the inherent values of metropolitan life and to suggest how they could be enhanced. If the metropolis is inevitable, we might also speculate on the form it should take and the facilities it should have, if this new way of living is to be the best man has yet enjoyed. The contributors were urged to explore the possibilities for action along two lines: the measures within our present reach and also those on the horizon that require an increase in our understanding or acceptance or that demand technical, economic, or administrative means not yet in existence.

The essays that follow represent the responses of a variety of specialists to the several aspects of this theme. Their discus-

sions touch on the possibilities of physical form, the technological restraints and potentials, and the economic, political,
social, and visual implications. They deal with the significance
of the metropolis for countries with modern economies and for
countries whose territory is underdeveloped. They consider
urban history, contemporary planning, and plausible aspirations for the future. Although the editors emphasized policy
and action, the statements range from the purely descriptive
and contemplative to cautious projection, utopian fancy, and
pragmatic recommendations for policy.

Certain essays recognize that leisure will increase along with
automation and that mobility will be the higher as facilities for
transportation and communication proliferate. Others expect
the metropolis to grow at the expense of the smaller cities. Yet
others emphasize the high cost of capital outlay and of maintenance, or such technical constraints as the limitations on open
space, the prospect of a water shortage, the difficult question of
pollution, the increasing overload on communication. One
paper touches on growing social stratification and the trend
toward relatively homogeneous neighborhoods. Another in-
terprets the varying patterns of individual participation in
community affairs; yet another, the sensitivity of the artist to
the increasing discomfort, the lack of order and meaning in
city life. Two final papers deal with the anti-urban attitude of
the American intellectual, and the city as it appears in the
literature of utopia.

On the whole these papers are optimistic, although they vary
in degree. None of the difficulties raised is considered in-
superable. In general, the metropolis is regarded as creating
fundamental opportunities for higher incomes, a greater variety
and a wider choice of modes of living, a way of life that could
be more stimulating, more enlightened, and more conducive to
innovations. There are many proposals for bringing about these
and other desirable goals.

At a meeting that brought together most of the authors and
a number of other experts, some of the issues implicit in these

papers were discussed. A summary of the chief points made at
the seminar will serve, we believe, as a useful introduction to
the various concepts and issues. Since all the papers agreed
that a basic goal of the future metropolis was to offer a wide
variety of choice in all the aspects of living and working, it
seemed appropriate to begin with an examination of this goal.
It soon became apparent that agreement was more apparent
than real: did choice refer to jobs, to style of living, to cultural
opportunities, or to all three? Was there any line of demarca-
tion at which increased choice had little meaning? Was it not
essential to measure the cost of choice, especially in terms of
sacrificing other opportunities? And how should this goal be
interpreted for persons or groups whose preferences are at
wide variance? Although no single answer to these questions
emerged, everyone acknowledged that the largest metropolis
provides the greatest variety in choice of jobs and probably
the maximum variety of cultural opportunities; but it is note-
worthy that no one considered that we have so far achieved
anything near an optimum variety of styles of living, including
an adequate range of environments with varying physical settings, activities, and social groups.

Nathan Glazer, staff member of the Joint Center for Urban
Studies, asked how to prevent what seventy percent of people
think they want from becoming what ninety-nine percent
actually obtain. Subsidy, either governmental or private, was
one answer, but subsidy implies additional constraints; nonetheless, this means was favored whenever it encouraged a real
variety. The issue, it was emphasized, was not between subsidy
and no subsidy (subsidies being already fairly widespread),
but whether the purpose of the subsidy was relevant and valid.
Oscar Handlin cited the subsidies indirectly supplied to the
automobile in the 1920's by the public highways, while the
development of rapid interurban trolleys was prevented by
taxation, the strict regulation of fares, and the lack of subsidy.

The seminar turned next to the problem of the "gray areas."
These are the areas Raymond Vernon and his colleagues have

dramatized by their investigations of the New York metropolitan region. According to their studies, both the metropolitan core and also the outlying suburbs are likely to undergo a substantial growth, regardless of future problems; but the intermediate or "gray areas" present an unsavory prospect of miles of minimum-standard housing. As income rises along with standards of demand, residents may be expected to move from these areas, while an influx of new families seems unlikely. It is equally improbable that these "gray areas" could be remodeled at costs and standards that permit sufficiently low rents or that they could be cleared for new uses without prohibitive costs far steeper than those now contemplated.

Some of the members of the seminar who had played a leading role in the 1930's in developing the national housing policy recounted the mistakes, perhaps inevitable, then committed. Aside from some ambitious reports and pious speeches, the "housers" at that time gave scant attention to the overriding challenge of the metropolis. Their measures had been particularized and pragmatic, and few had expected standard accommodations to be made available in any quantity within the reach of the moderate-income family. No one had reckoned with a change in economic conditions or with a revolution in the financing terms of home ownership. Today we observe many middle- and low-income families moving to the suburbs and leaving behind them the perplexing problem of the "gray areas."

Hardly anyone at the seminar saw any utopian possibilities or any quick and easy solutions. These "gray areas" could conceivably be converted to serve as highly accessible air terminals or even as rural retreats in town, for there is a dearth of nearby inexpensive resorts where individuals or families may go for play or relaxation.

The role of technology in constructing the future metropolis was next considered. People are always adjusting to the technological innovations that spring from individual need or effort. Suppose, we remarked, that all society were the client, instead of a few persons or firms; and suppose we could devise whatever technology was desired, at a reasonable cost—what kind of innovations should we then seek in order to make the future course of metropolitan development a happier one? Our technology has been reasonably successful in developing the kinds of weapons and space devices requested. Can we not count on at least a modest success in other directions as well?

This question was examined with some care and a number of technological improvements were called for, such as those which would permit replacing personal journeys by messages, or which would allow the building of self-contained houses free of utility connections, or which would produce small cars the size of a bus seat, which could hook on and off a larger vehicle. Some persons, however, were skeptical of the potentials for prefabrication. Perhaps the leading recommendation, advanced, to be sure, with restrained optimism, was to increase the efficiency, attractiveness, and prestige of public transportation so as to provide an effective competition with the private passenger car. Another proposal was to treat investments in communication and transportation, not as costs that automatically are held as low as possible, but rather as an efficient means of controlling urban density, form, and growth, and for giving the variety of choice in living and working its highest possible expression for all groups in the community.

The final session of the seminar turned to some aspects of policymaking as related to metropolitan form and growth. Everyone agreed that there will be an enormous expansion in physical plant and population, both in the poorer and in the more advanced economies. The former have less funds, fewer qualified specialists, and a less mature system of cities, but they do have a greater degree of governmental control over development and fewer ideological restraints in applying control. The crucial question was how policy should influence growth, if at all. Does it make sense, as one paper proposes, to divert the migration from rural areas to new metropolitan centers? To turn to another paper, which of the various hypothetical forms, whether pure or mixed, should be adopted? The discussion assumed that the pattern of growth could be a variable, subject to control, and sought convincing reasons for favoring any one pattern.

Italian and Soviet experience was marshalled to illustrate the failure of direct efforts to restrict the influx of population to a major metropolis. The discussants also brought out the importance of the market, the availability of suppliers, labor force, consumers, and business services to account for the migration of firms and families to the big cities, aside from the heightened competition and the variety of opportunity in such cities. Everyone conceded, however, that some situations call for a contrary flow; one example is the successful shift of the Turkish capital from Istanbul to Ankara, which not only buttressed Turkish political and military objectives, but also eased the problems of developing Istanbul. Other examples were cited, such as United States policy in developing the West in the nineteenth century, Soviet Russia's recent expansion in the Urals, and the present efforts of the Venezuelan government to diversify the economy by constructing a vast industrial complex in the Orinoco-Caroni region. Karl W. Deutsch also pointed out that in the United States, Great Britain, and Germany (the three countries with the greatest growth in the nineteenth century) the urban pattern included several large centers rather than one single major city.

The group agreed that wherever such objectives exist there are also methods to help deflect the flow of population, particularly to alternative large centers. The Puerto Ricans, for instance, need not go only to New York City; if they are aided with information and subsidies for transportation, they could be diverted to other centers of economic opportunity. The pattern of the flow of population could be influenced by the pattern of the transportation system, such as the railroads in the United States in the last century, or by investment in basic community equipment and services. The opening up of new regions might contribute to a new pattern of growth and perhaps in time to the decentralization of political power—a problem the less developed countries will probably have to wrestle with in the coming decades.

In conclusion, the seminar discussed some possible forms of the future metropolis and the reasons for preferring any one to another. A maximum flexibility of choice, ease of circulation, and minimum cost were judged the most important criteria; others were the relative capacity for growth and the minimal burden on the transport and control mechanisms. In most of the poorer countries today, such usual or desirable urban forms as that of the star, the linear pattern, and the doughnut were likely to be impracticable because of the difficulty in controlling the invasion of publicly owned open space by squatters. This problem could be eased if defined areas were set aside for squatters, so that controls could be humane and effective as well as rational. The general consensus was that the polynuclear grid system described in one of the articles in this issue was probably far superior in satisfying the above criteria. Oddly enough, it was noted, of all the forms considered this one most nearly approaches present urban patterns.

Planning and dreaming are old pastimes. When applied to cities, plans and dreams have usually been aimed at solving problems of the present or at inducing a return to some image of the past: expressways were devised to escape the traffic jam, slum clearance to solve the housing problem, while neighborhood development looks back to the small community, and Broadacre City to the family farm. Only rarely do we find a contemporary plan that anticipates the future with pleasure. Men are attracted to the metropolis by real values—choice, freedom, privacy, opportunity, culture, entertainment. How can we ensure the realization of these ends? More importantly, what are the possibilities for metropolitan life that are as yet undreamed of? And what kind of power, knowledge, or guidance must be applied to achieve them? The spirit of hopeful intervention should prove at least as effective as the desire to escape present discomfort.

2. *The Social System*

OSCAR HANDLIN

WE STAND AT a point in time strategically convenient for an examination of the social structure of the contemporary city. Every indication points to the fact that we have recently come to the end of one period of urban development and are moving on into another. From this vantage point it will be useful to review the significant developments of the past with an eye to discerning the probable patterns of the future. What character the society of the emerging city is likely to take may be perceived by an analysis of the history of that which it is replacing.

This examination is focused on the experience of the American city, partly because information on it was more readily available, partly because it seemed to be quite representative of what happened in western society generally. The unique characteristics commonly attributed to the cities of the United States proved, upon closer analysis, to be such as were only more visible there than elsewhere. Their recent origin sometimes gave the surface impression that they rose from the wilderness full-grown and without social antecedents. That the foreign-born formed so large a part of their population seemed to make them exceptional polyglot melting pots. Yet while Berlin or Vienna or Milan had ancient origins, the modern communities that bear those names are as new as those of New York or Boston. And the residents of the continental cities were drawn from fully as wide a range of social and cultural backgrounds as those of the American ones. In the case of Europe continuity of formal institutions and of political insti-

tutions covered up developments that occurred in the open
and in a more extreme form in the United States; but the social
experience was analogous enough to justify the concentration
of attention in this paper upon the cities of the New World.

This discussion will not begin, in the usual manner, with an
effort to define and analyze the class structure of the city. It
will be more useful, rather, first to establish the historical context of the problem and then to trace the forms within which
urban residents at various periods organized themselves to
pursue common goals. That will offer a framework within
which change can be estimated and evaluated.

At the opening of the eighteenth century, all western cities
bore the recognizable signs of their medieval origins. Circumscribed in area by the necessities of walled defensive systems,
they rarely held more than 25,000 inhabitants and their social
order had the formal corporate simplicity of communities in
which status was externally defined, totally recognizable, and
permanently fixed. Only London by then had begun to display
more modern characteristics. Other cities grew in population
after 1700 but did not change their character until later.

Apart from London, the modern city is a product of the
nineteenth century. The complex forces that transformed it are
conveniently summarized by the term industrialization. On the
economic plane they included: the elaboration of transportation networks to carry an enormously expanded volume of
goods which passed through the city, where they were handled,
serviced, exchanged, and accounted for; the creation of territorially large market areas around a metropolitan nucleus; the
mechanization of manufacturing and its shift to an urban setting; and the growth of administrative functions located in the
city. There followed a radical widening of geographical limits,
a phenomenal increase in population, the appearance of entirely new social groups, and a profound alteration in the physical conditions of urban life. These changes destroyed the social

order inherited from the medieval town and called for altogether new adjustments.

In the last two decades there have been meaningful signs that the western city has moved into another process of transformation. Changes in the character of manufacturing and of the labor force, new patterns of income distribution and family life, and a cultural style dominated by the technology of the automobile and the mass media have altered significantly the ways in which organized groups took form in the city, the character of their leadership, the incidence of conflicts among them, and the elements making for disorganization and individuality. Those are the basic elements that established the social system of the modern city.

THE CAPACITY FOR SOCIAL ACTION

The central social problem of the city was that of developing the means through which the great agglomerations of humanity assembled there could act toward personal or common goals. At the opening of the eighteenth century, cities still revealed their medieval origin, not only in their fortified walls and their physical layouts but also in their social structure, the basic elements of which were corporate communal organizations. Whether these were formally embodied in guilds and confraternities as in Europe, or more loosely structured as in America, each was an entity that comprehended a complex of functions. Knit together by kinship, localized in a definable residential district, and possessed of both an occupational and a religious nexus, each group enjoyed a status defined by custom and law and supported by distinctive privileges and immunities.

Not all the residents of the city were citizens. Above the accepted social order, there lived a body of men who represented political power—royal officials, officers of the garrison, and noblemen who maintained establishments there out of the desire either to be close to the centers of authority or to escape the isolation of their estates or to enjoy the pleasures of town life. Outside the accepted social order also were a multitude of inferior men. The Jews lived in ghettoes or outside the walls; and frequently enclaves of foreign traders were tolerated in their own compounds under their own laws. In addition a floating population of seamen and strangers and of servants and journeymen without masters was grudgingly permitted to lodge in the town. These men occupied an anomalous situation, for the community disapproved of the presence of such as were not firmly located in a household that was part of a recognized responsible group.

In the eighteenth century the addition of large numbers of the placeless elements weakened this antique social order. There was, furthermore, a general loss of confidence in the authority of established institutions that, by the end of the century, would produce the near-revolutionary mobs ready to burst into disorder.

The American cities anticipated the European in these developments. A high rate of social and geographic mobility inhibited the development of a firm institutional structure. It proved impossible to establish guild organizations, and apprenticeship regulations quickly broke down. Groupings tended to follow occupational lines and fell into such gross categories as merchants or artisans; and in many activities even those distinctions were not respected. Significantly, such outsiders as the Jews were yielded places as citizens.

Furthermore, the aristocratic-military governing group was small and weak and quickly relinquished power over the city to its citizens. The struggle that in Europe involved a bitter and not always successful battle, in the New World was won almost by default. But in all western cities, by the last quarter of the eighteenth century, there were evident signs of the decay of the old medieval order.

The economic changes of the late eighteenth and nineteenth centuries immensely furthered these tendencies. The expanded functions of the city in transportation, commerce, industry, and administration made room for a steadily rising population that rendered inherited social forms anachronistic.

The rapid increase was largely a product of immigration. Everywhere the children of residents formed a diminishing element in the total population, an ever larger part of which was composed of newcomers. In the United States the new arrivals were largely foreign-born. But it was not the change in nationality that contributed most to their strangeness. Differences in language, habits and aspirations set them off from the earlier inhabitants; and in that respect they were similar to the peasants who were at the same time entering the European cities. The diversity of origins was everywhere a complicating factor.

Under the pressure of a rising population, the city spread territorially. The increase in the number of residents, the loss of the military values of the walls, and the development of transit facilities, all these factors encouraged the city to expand far beyond its older limits, swallowing up in the process the agricultural villages and the smaller urban places in the neighborhood.

The increase in population and territorial expansion both influenced the internal society in the city. The immense dimensions of these communities created new problems of organization and control. The diversity of origins of the population, its greater numbers, and the wider spaces within which it was housed in themselves set individuals and single families adrift and made it difficult to live within customary forms.

But in any case, the most important of those forms could not be transplanted to, or preserved in, the new city because of the fragmentation of the traditional household. Earlier, the workshop of the artisan and the counting houses of the merchant, like the farm of the husbandman, had been an all-encompassing entity within which were united familial, religious, and economic activities. The situation of each individual in the larger community had been located with reference to his position in a given household. Now the complex occupational organization of the city detached the individual from the household and isolated him in an impersonal relationship to his employment. Increasingly, a man's calling, whether in factory, office or craft, was altogether independent of other aspects of his existence. Large numbers came together for stated periods of the day to work, and then scattered individually to a multitude of districts, where they lived in a variety of types of houses without relationship among the family, religious, or social organizations that occupied the other periods of their lives. The earlier corporate urban social structure therefore quickly became anachronistic. The old forms vanished or, where they persisted, survived merely as antique curiosities.

If these organizations were to be replaced at all, it would be by entirely new ones. The municipality and its related institutions rapidly lost contact with the vast majority of the city's population, who were no longer even connected to it as taxpayers. It performed no function in their lives and supplied them with no services except ritual and ornamental ones, which, as outsiders, they did not value. When such people sought to act on their own behalf they looked for altogether new devices to enable them to do so.

A large, although indeterminate, part of the population never really succeeded in creating new forms to take the place of the old. They constituted a drifting, isolated mass, the elements of which belonged to no larger group. Such men and women never actually managed to establish roots in the city. They lived alone in their flats, lost contact with their kinfolk, and died in obscurity.

Others immediately attempted to reconstruct some larger social entity and, since it could not be all-encompassing, did so by contriving means of satisfying the particular needs that the old household and the community of which it had been a part had satisfied comprehensively. They thus developed the characteristic social unit of the modern city—a voluntary association dedicated to the performance of some specific function in the lives of its members.

Such associations appeared in a multitude of guises. They were distinguished by no elements of uniformity other than that of their common emphasis upon a limited, concrete, rather than a broad, general function. The new societies maintained places for worship or cared for the ill, or buried the dead, or offered mutual aid, or provided educational, fraternal or recreational facilities. All these were characteristically particular rather than general in their operations. And it is in the development of these organizations, rather than of any inclusive class structure, that one finds the key to the social system of the nineteenth-century city.

The degree to which men were capable of forming such organizations varied markedly from society to society and depended upon the political, cultural, and social setting in which they existed. In the United States the looseness and feebleness of inherited institutions and the already existing habits of pluralism encouraged the spread of these associations in a wide and diverse range of activities. Elsewhere the existence of established churches or of other strongly entrenched institutions was an inhibiting factor. So too, the extent to which the state was permissive or intolerant in its control over the internal life of the city shaped the scope of operations of the voluntary association. But everywhere whatever capacity for common action existed took this form.

These associations, however, did not exist in complete detachment from one another. Although they were separate entities, overlapping membership, common economic and social interests, and the persistent influence of common origins provided the basis for wider communal alignments. Within a territorially discrete district, a neighborhood or *quartier*, men were sometimes likely to be associated in the same complex of activities. In the same way ethnic connections were often likely to draw individuals into the same societies. The neighborhood and the ethnic group were not tightly organized institutions; more properly speaking, they were limits within which the associational activities of their members were likely to fall.

In those cities, as in the United States, in which distinctly recognized differences of origin clearly set off the various segments of the incoming population, the ethnic groupings acquired a particularly binding character, for they alone furnished an element of continuity between one generation and another. The lines of common descent, presumed or actual, provided a matrix within which the group organized its policing devices, family life, marriage, churches, educational system, and associations for cultural and social ends. Within the group there was room for considerable differentiation and for internal pluralism; for what held it together was not its uniformity or coherence but the commonly recognized limits of its membership.

Nor was the ethnic group automatically or simply formed as a product of differences in traits originally brought into the city. It came into being only when those differences were recognized and given social weight. Thus in the United States some groups did not discover their own identity until well after their settlement. Even more enlightening is the dissimilar experience of people who migrated to different societies. The Irish became extremely self-conscious in Boston or New York or Glasgow but much less so in London or in Liverpool. Spaniards who went to Havana maintained an awareness of provincial peculiarities much more than those who went to Madrid. The dominant social assumptions of the receiving city could thus either emphasize or obscure ethnic identification.

In situations in which the ethnic group was important, it usually overshadowed the neighborhood, which appeared as urban growth made room for a diversified residential pattern. In the United States, the various districts of the city quickly acquired an ethnic character. Differences in time of arrival and the clustering of institutions and services that attracted similar newcomers gave a predominant ethnic tone to each area of the city.

In cities in which the ethnic element was subordinate, on the other hand, the neighborhood acquired an identity and quality of its own and itself defined the ambit of group life. Ecological factors, the type of housing available, and location in relationship to the rest of the city then acquired predominant importance.

This framentation of the modes for social action among numerous particular organizations was a source of continual discontent. It seemed to deprive the city as a whole of order and direction. All the difficulties of urban life in the nineteenth century were ascribed to the resultant chaos and lack of control. The remedy most usually proposed was some form of integration, imposed externally by the state if need be.

But whether any degree of remedial integration was possible or not depended upon the character of the cities' economic development and upon the style of life it permitted the population housed in them. The great majority of urban residents in the nineteenth and twentieth centuries had originated in the countryside and, in migration, brought with them rural habits and modes of action. How they adjusted depended largely upon their situation in the productive system.

Only the well-entrenched aristocracies achieved an approximate extension of their old style of life under the new conditions. Not wholly committed to the city and retaining their seats in the hinterland, they were able to preserve the integrity of family and household forms, to treat their residence in the town as transient and to maintain a considerable distance between themselves and the problems of urban life. Walled houses, a closed society, and privileges that still commanded respect provided them with retreats from which they could enjoy the pleasures of town or court and execute such administrative tasks as they wished, but to which they withdrew in detachment from the difficulties the citizens encountered.

For that reason the aristocracy had relatively slight influence upon other elements of the urban population. In the United States it did not exist; efforts to form such a group artificially toward the end of the nineteenth century had little effect. But even in Vienna or Paris, the gentry were important in two respects only: they were consumers of goods and services, and they supplied a model of behavior for the possessors of mercantile and industrial wealth.

Apart from the aristocracy it made little sense to talk of a formal class system in the nineteenth-century city. The great mass of the urban population consisted of the families of laborers, whose incomes always left them dependent and insecure. An ever larger number were proletarians. Others worked on the docks, in the streets, in construction gangs, at home with the needle, as domestics or in service. In all these occupations earnings were low, so that the family maintained itself only through the labor of several members and through underconsumption. In all, employment was casual, from day to day, so that the worker lacked any security in his job. These depressed economic conditions carried with them inferior social status. Cut off and isolated, these people had little hope of escape either by a rise where they were or by further migration. They were also isolated by the lack of a definable human relationship to the city as a whole. Without property or a stake in the economy, they could not connect their own welfare with that of the metropolis and remained, as it were, permanent transients.

While they too therefore were eager to regain the wholeness of the rural communities they had left in coming to the city, they could perceive no practical means of doing so. They were rather compelled to confine themselves to the limited objectives attainable through voluntary associations within ethnic or neighborhood lines. Apart from that there was little possibility that they could achieve a more comprehensive and more satisfying social order.

Above this sector of the population there existed a broad spectrum of occupations which gave those in them some stake in the city. There were enormous differences of income, attitude and ethnic affiliation among the clerks and managers, shopkeepers and independent craftsmen, and merchants and professional men. But they enjoyed incomes large enough to permit the family to get by with the earnings of the head of the household. There was therefore a basis for considerable family cohesion and discipline, and the margin for some effort to satisfy their aspirations for a more stable social order.

The wealthiest aped the aristocracy and penetrated its ranks. But most had neither such ambitions nor the means to satisfy them. Their aims were more modest—to establish a stable family life, in a secure household, situated in an orderly community.

In a few places, like Paris, where the traditions of artisan life retained some degree of strength and continuity, it was possible to pursue these ideals within the confines of a slightly expanded city. But in most places where the bulk of population had rural antecedents, realization of these objectives called for a reconstruction in the urban context of the rural community. The result was the growth of the suburbs. The movement to the periphery of the cities by families whose breadwinners continued to work at its center began toward the middle of the nineteenth century, made possible by the development of transit systems, by the separation of employment from residence and by the growing desire to reconstruct the values of the rural community.

The suburb was thus a special kind of neighborhood. Often, particularly in the United States, it had a defined ethnic character. But more important, it supplied a setting in which it was possible to attempt to reestablish old rural patterns. Church organization, single-family houses, a rustic town plan that preserved spaces of greenery, and a disciplined surveillance of personal life all reflected the intention of creating a homogeneous community rooted in the practices of the past. Such communities had the incidental, but consequential, virtue, of course, of securing some degree of detachment from the most difficult problems of the city proper.

The suburban style of life, however, involved severe strains. The separation in experience of the head of the household from the rest of the family created serious psychological problems. Furthermore, the divorce between place of residence and place of occupation entailed great costs, some of which, as in transportation, were borne by others, but much of which formed a heavy fixed charge against family income.

It was very difficult therefore to achieve a satisfactory suburban life. Success depended upon money, transportation and the ability of those of common background to sort themselves out without excessive compulsion. Furthermore, it was rarely possible to preserve the stability of a suburban situation for as long as a whole generation. The continuing growth of the city rapidly engulfed district after district so that the respectable suburb of one decade was frequently well on the way toward becoming a slum in the next. In the nineteenth and twentieth centuries, therefore, only a small portion of the total urban population could use this means of restoring order and stability to their social life.

Among the unpropertied elements who could not escape to the suburbs, more comprehensive forms of action developed only rarely. In some places the labor union encompassed a variety of activities that extended out from the laborer in relationship to his job to broader political, social and cultural concerns. Elsewhere political organizations, such as the machines in the cities of the United States, showed a similar capacity for providing a nucleus of coherent communal action. But such alternatives were feasible only when the people involved maintained some degree of fixity in their jobs and in their residences.

Otherwise the social system remained fragmented, with large parts of the population able to act only toward the limited goals that their own associations could achieve. In the United States, where voluntarism, pluralism and diversity were already characteristic, that led to a fluid group life with considerable capacity for adjusting to the needs of many different elements. But where external forces or inherited institutions inhibited the effective organization of the propertyless, they often remained immobilized and helpless.

Since the Second World War new forces seem clearly to be at work to alter the character of urban group life. In the last fifteen years, there has been a radical transformation in the income structure of the large city. A general rise in real wage levels and a shrinkage in the requirements for unskilled labor have liquidated a large part of the former proletariat and altered the situation of that which remains. The marginal wage earners now are largely employed outside the city or, within it, comprise small groups of recent arrivals.

The sector of the urban population that can aspire to propertied status has therefore expanded rapidly. Yet these people have not thereby increased their capacity for social action; indeed they have lowered it. The suburb has become less effective as a community than earlier. The automobile and the developing highway network have enabled ever larger numbers to move away from the center of the city. But the suburb now exists within quite an altered social context.

The present population of the cities is less clearly linked to rural antecedents than that of the past. Spatial mobility remains a prominent characteristic of contemporary life; and the cities still continue annually to receive a substantial body of immigrants. But an ever-increasing percentage of them are people with urban backgrounds, for whom the ideal of the rural community has little direct attraction. This is altogether apart from the fact that other forces by now have had a disintegrating impact upon the rural communities themselves.

As a result, the new suburbanites do not bring with them a clearly patterned image, derived from their own past, of what they wish their communities to be like. Their motives in escaping are largely negative—to avoid undesirable aspects of urban life. Furthermore, with the disappearance or decline of the aristocracy they have lost their only alternative model for emulation. For the positive features of their communities they draw neither on their own personal experiences in a remembered rural past nor on the visible example of a superior group. Rather they depend on impressions loosely derived from the mass media, which have become an ever more important source of their ideals. Indeed, those standards are often pre-built into the structure of real-estate developments, just as are other appliances. The difficulty is that those ideals are concerned largely with external physical features; they have little relevance to the authentic experiences of those who have come to the suburbs in the last two decades.

The propertyless laborers who remain in the central city face other problems. Although their relative percentage in the total population is declining and although their income is rising, the gap between what they desire and what they have remains as large as ever, for their expectations have been growing. They are therefore still discontented. Furthermore, they feel constricted by the increasing power of impersonal institutions over which they have little control—not only the government and the corporations for which they work, but also the unions of which they are members and the housing projects in which they reside.

Changes, general to all levels of the city's population, have also affected voluntary group life. The altered income structure of the population, the growing prominence of the government in matters related to social security and public welfare, and the increasing bureaucratization of philanthropy have circumscribed the area within which spontaneous activities can take place. The fraternal, benevolent and mutual aid associations have given way to the impersonal agencies of the state or of the community chests and united funds, in which the participation of laymen is largely limited to the solicitation of funds. The annual contribution is in the nature of a tax and calls for no active involvement as the older societies did.

The neighborhood and the ethnic group have also lost some of their capacity for supplying a meaningful matrix for communal activity. Whole districts of the older cities have been physically obliterated, either through the war in Europe, or through slum clearance and new construction in the United States. In the process of rebuilding, old neighborhoods have freqently lost their identity and now share with newer districts a general colorless sameness. Ethnic groupings have also declined in vitality except insofar as they have been converted into religious forms dedicated to preserving family order. Only when they are externally strengthened by color consciousness or prejudice do they function as vigorously as before.

Increasingly, in the past two decades, the activities of the urban population have been concentrated on the coherence and unity of the family. To a considerable and growing degree, organized communal life, particularly in the suburbs, is child-centered and revolves about the institutions which will preserve the nest within which offspring are reared. That accounts for the great concern with education and the schools. It also explains the growing importance of church membership. The fact that the government now can play little or no role in religious matters has left this sphere of social activity particularly open to voluntary organization. But in addition the rise in the membership of religious institutions reflects the desire to use them as a source of discipline, tradition and authority. This has been strikingly characteristic of the United States, but also of France, Italy and Germany.

The growth of the contemporary suburbs has thus been only symptomatic of broader social changes in the life of the city. Lacking firmly fixed personal or social goals and swayed by the imprecise standards communicated through the mass media, large parts of its population have lost the capacity for acting meaningfully in groups, except when it comes to matters which touch immediately upon their family life. Outside these narrow personal concerns there has been a perceptible decline in the capacity for group action.

LEADERSHIP IN THE MODERN CITY

The diminishing capacity for group action in the modern city has complicated all the problems in the relationship of leadership to its following. The capacity of groups to act was, in the past, manifested through exceptional individuals who expressed their objectives and formulated the strategy through which those ends were to be attained. The changes of the last two decades have seriously weakened the role of communal leaders.

In the earliest towns the structure of authority was conditioned by the fact that power was external, resting in the hands of governmental and military officials and functionaries superior to the whole body of citizens. But the indigenous urban population, while inferior, had its own recognized officialdom of mayors, aldermen and other dignitaries.

With the decay of corporate communal institutions in the nineteenth century, the holders of formal municipal office lost a good deal of their importance. They no longer spoke for the organized sectors of the population and they still lacked effective power as against the officials of the nation or the state. The fact that the magistrates of the city were chosen by an expanding electorate did not add to their authority. They played a role that was primarily ceremonial and were charged with only a narrow range of administrative functions. It was rare rather than usual for mayors to be among the genuine leaders of the urban community, and when they were, it was only by virtue of some exceptional personal circumstance.

Effective leadership in the nineteenth-century city was generated by its multitude of organizations. Each association had its recognized roster of officers, each neighborhood its known men of distinction in whose leadership defined circles of followers acquiesced. There was of course considerable variation from country to country, in the extent to which such activities were tolerated or encouraged. But everywhere they were the soil within which the seeds of leadership germinated.

Given the recency of arrival of most of the city's population, leadership, like organized activity, was likely to be disposed within ethnic lines. The choice was apt to fall upon particularly mobile individuals who, while familiar with their following, were also able to deal with the larger world of the city about them. But there were times also when the leader appeared from outside the group, from the marginal elements capable of acting as its intermediaries.

The communal leaders were thus drawn from or related to, but not identical with, their followings. Many were intellectuals whose command of communications enabled them to address and to listen to large sectors of the population. Clergymen and journalists thus knew how to give comprehensible form to the ideas of masses of men not familiar with the use of words. Lawyers who had contact with government and knowledge of procedures were also in a strategic position. And occasionally businessmen had the leisure and wealth to devote to these concerns.

Urban leadership was therefore neither unified nor coherent, but fragmented. A more comprehensive leadership developed only in the organized labor movement and in politics, fields in which the concerns of a variety of groups were mingled. But more generally leadership remained dispersed. In that chaotic but nevertheless fluid and flexible situation, the participants in every activity could find some guidance. Only the apathetic, inactive and unorganized remained unled.

This situation also offered useful channels for communication and negotiation among the various groups in the city. Horizontal links among the leaders developed common attitudes and interests; and the relationship of each to his own following permitted him to act as mediator between his own group and others.

In recent decades, the expanded scale of urban life, the dispersal of residence, the sense of remoteness of individuals from one another, and the decay of many aspects of group activity, have weakened the apparatus by which leaders and followers formerly established contact with one another. Furthermore, the growing importance of government and particularly of national government in the lives of the urban masses has shifted attention away from the local and familiar to the re-

mote but powerful. Government has ceased to be simply the
distant source of authority. It collects taxes, pays welfare benefits, conscripts sons, and polices the personal affairs of the
citizens far more intimately than ever before. And as these
activities have grown in weight at the expense of local ones,
the mass of citizens are increasingly likely to define leadership
in distant rather than immediate terms. There cannot be in
this relationship the same rapport there was in the old one;
the character of the communications is different. The leader
can speak to his following, but he cannot listen to it; public
opinion polls in this respect have not supplied an equivalent
for the sensitivity of the participant in shared experiences.

The distance between leader and following is widened by
the almost total monopoly of the means of communication held
by mass media which have established a direct connection between the individual and the vague but familiar figures recognized from television or from the national magazine. These
media can indeed generate an intense sense of loyalty and
attachment to the great leader but they do not provide the
following with the capacity to communicate directly with him.
On the other hand, the development of the mass media and
the increasingly consistent focus of attention upon them have
weakened the connection between the individual and the
groups in the society closest to him. It therefore becomes increasingly difficult to establish firm leadership or to find a
direct basis for action on this level.

INDIVIDUAL AND INTERGROUP TENSIONS

The changing internal social order of the city significantly
influenced both the place of the individual in it and the relationships of various groups to one another. In no period did
the organized sectors of the population exist simply in free-
floating isolation; their contacts with one another and with
their members sometimes created tensions that called for
resolution either through conflict or adjustment.

In the medieval towns, the corporate character of the

groups and of the households within them permitted an hierarchical structure, places in which were determined by proximity to the external sources of power. Since that proximity was in turn closely related to wealth and economic status, the resultant social structure was uncomplicated and orderly. Everyone occupied a totally defined place as well as a totally defined status and was governed by a recognized code of conduct. Disputes arose only between factions within a given group, except during periods of social and economic strain when inferior elements were temporarily able to challenge the power and authority of superior ones. Personal delinquency created few problems so long as each individual was located in, and accountable to, a fixed household and a fixed group.

The growth of the modern city complicated and obscured the relationships of the urban population to the sources of outside power. At first the well-established, well-entrenched elements permitted the incursion of large numbers of new inhabitants without serious efforts to control them. The merchants and artisans, and later the manufacturers, utilized the cheap labor of the fresh arrivals without any sense of threat to their own security and without oversight. The well-to-do simply protected themselves against the possibilities of theft or attack by the force of their own, or by hired, arms.

In the nineteenth century, when this tolerant and permissive attitude disappeared, it still remained difficult for any group to establish effective control in the city. The old officials had lost their authority and their ability to command as the institutions they represented became anachronistic.

For a long time nothing took their place. The absence of competent police forces prevented close supervision of large parts of the city. These problems of law enforcement were long insurmountable. Because of the dense conditions of residence and the anonymity of a large part of the population, individual transgressors could not readily be identified and tracked down. When they had the support of organized groups they were practically unreachable. It was a long time before effective techniques of policing were devised.

Furthermore, there was a widespread reluctance to create this new kind of power, the character and control of which were necessarily uncertain. The state and the citizens were often at odds with one another in the nineteenth century and hesitant about bringing into being forces that might unpredictably throw their weight one way or the other. Those fears were intensified to the extent that the new elements in the population began to demand a share of power.

Under these conditions, extensive regions of the city were abandoned to their own devices. There the nominal officials had no power, the nominal law did not run. Violence was endemic and the only social controls were such as were supported by the sanctions of local associations, locally led. The established citizenry desired only to protect itself from contagion.

After mid-century, however, no *cordon sanitaire* was effective. Not only did the masses occasionally emerge from the slums as a mob, threatening all values, but the constant intercourse between upper and lower levels of the population became a running menace to the security of the property and health of all. Finally, as the masses developed autonomous organizations of their own, they began to reach for power in the vacuum of municipal political life.

The result was persistent tension that frequently exploded into open conflict, the forms of which varied with the social and cultural conditions of the communities involved. The divisions and the consequent struggles for control might be oriented along occupational or along ethnic lines; they might be channeled within political or economic contests. But in one way or another, they arrayed the developing groups of the city against one another.

The fright of the established, propertied elements reflected the gravity of the situation. The specter of the commune haunted the comfortable burghers, in deference to whom armories were built at commanding points and new streets laid out with a view to effective defense.

More important was the determination to achieve more

effective control. After mid-century there was increasing emphasis on the development of the police, recruited generally from the masses but gradually endowed with more effective techniques of operation. By the 1880's there were significant experiments with means of registering and identifying the whole population and with extending the force of law into every district of the city.

Parallel to the mobilization of that power was an effort in many communities to generate social obedience and discipline. Various forms of discrimination were the means of establishing the social inferiority of some groups to others. The extension of public education was also regarded as a means of persuading the populace to accept the conception of order and the norms of behavior defined by the groups that sought dominance. Philanthropy often served the same purpose. Without in the least minimizing the humanitarian or religious impulses that drew individuals into charitable activities, it is nevertheless true that those activities also had a disciplinary and educational function. They defined the superior position of the benefactor and the inferiority of the recipient; and they confirmed the validity of the former's norm of behavior. By the same token, they identified as delinquency such behavior as deviated from the standards of the dominant groups— poverty and its concomitants, failures to conform to accepted patterns of personal life, and defiance of the law.

In the twentieth century, the essential situation remained unchanged. The drive to establish control continued, supported by the growing technical efficiency of the police system. But large sectors of the city's population remained undisciplined, either subject to no rule at all or governed by autonomous organizations which reflected the inability or unwillingness of the submerged groups to accept the standards and the authority of the superior ones.

This situation offered considerable latitude to the noncomforming individual who could escape in the interstices of the loose social order. The feeble means of identification allowed

rascals, artists and marginal characters of various sorts to drift
through the city's life without affiliation and with but slight
external control.

The changes of recent decades have increased order and
control, have lowered intergroup tension, and have put a growing pressure upon the individual to conform to ever more
widely accepted norms of behavior.

The constant improvement of police techniques has been
supplemented by more refined methods of registration supplied
by the state. These provided more effective means of identification than any of the old systems of *cartes d'identités* or pass-
ports because they enlisted the cooperation of the subjects
themselves. Social security, for instance, established a compulsory benefit for maintaining an identification which was
also a precondition of employment. The extension of direct
taxation to every wage earner and the requirements of various
systems for universal liability to conscription had the same
effect. As a result it has become increasingly more difficult to
maintain any degree of anonymity even in the largest and most
densely settled cities.

Moreover, the steady rise in income levels has added to the
number of citizens with a stake in social order. The laborer
who comes to own his own home or car acquires a property
interest, in defense of which he will often become quite sympathetic with complaints against high taxes and excessive expenditures. He is less likely to be drawn into unruly or
mob-like actions and more likely to look for guidance to the
well-established propertied elements in the community.

To the extent that a larger sector of the population is now
housed in the suburbs, the potentialities for control are also
extended. The means for identification and discipline are far
more effective there than in the central city; and the uniform
character of these places makes them susceptible in a large
measure to identical pressures and surveillance.

Finally, the weakening of many forms of autonomous group

life deprives the individual of alternatives. As the avenues of escape narrow, the more he is left with but one standard to which to conform. The loss of local leadership and the growing influence of the mass media have the same effects.

The result has been a steady lowering of intergroup tensions. Economic issues have become impersonal, resolved by large organizations within which the individual exercises relatively slight influence and the goals of which are some form of accommodation rather than open conflict. Nor are questions rooted in ethnic differences any longer likely to lead to serious divisions. Here too the most active organizations grow more are more alike and seek common grounds for accommodation.

Only the intractable problems created by color still remain divisive, particularly in the United States, in England, and in South Africa. The groupings of which color is the visible evidence are not readily dissolved, especially since they are still coterminous with profound economic, social and cultural differences. Furthermore, the colored residents of the city, more than any others, remain confined to the central slums and to occupations with low earning power and are least exposed to the influence of the suburbs and of the prosperity likely to instill a desire for order and stability. In some localities there are signs of a willingness to make room even for these people that may provide a basis for abatement of the tensions between them and the whites; but there is everywhere still a long way to go before this strain is eliminated. Apart from this exception, however, the city has achieved a greater degree of internal order, with less social tension, than ever before in its modern history.

On the other hand, the basic causes of individual tension have not been eliminated; indeed, in some respects they are more grave. The pressures toward conformity have increased as the mediating institutions which formerly stood between the individual and the whole community have grown feebler. There are not as many groups now within which the person whose heritage, habits or personality prevent him from conforming may take refuge. Any deviation is increasingly likely to be considered a form of delinquency.

The violations which stem from poverty and ignorance have decidedly declined in the past two decades and are now largely confined to such marginal groups as still occupy depressed social and economic positions. On the other hand, transgressions of the codes of personal behavior and difficulties in habituating adolescents to an acceptance of those codes have probably increased, in reflection of the greater rigidity of social norms and the extreme demands upon the individual for acquiescence. These developments no doubt reflect resentment against the contraction of the range of individual choices which is part of the price of growing social stability in the city.

The stupendous growth of the modern city in the nineteenth century destroyed the old hierarchical order based on the defined relationships of corporately organized households. The social system that then emerged was loosely structured through a large number of autonomous and scarcely articulated associations. The disorder of that situation in some ways added to the problems of expansion. But it provided a viable means through which large populations could act together toward immediate goals under unfamiliar conditions. It also left a good deal of latitude to the individual who could select among alternative modes of affiliation or take the risk of isolation and anonymity. That no doubt contributed substantially to the creativity of urban communities.

In the last two decades that situation has been changing. Many of the immediate associations and groupings have lost their vitality or have disappeared; and the surviving modes of social action are mostly such as are large and formally organized. The individual thus confronts, with fewer intermediaries than before, a massive social order which offers him relatively few choices and often makes excessive demands on him for conformity to patterns of behavior over which he has little control.

The elimination of the violence, disorder and social tension of the nineteenth-century city has certainly been a gain. But whether the capacity for free decisions and creative action was thereby necessarily diminished or not is still an open question. A good deal will depend upon whether or not the surrounding society in which the city is situated will encourage, tolerate, or discourage efforts to find a contemporary equivalent.

3. *The Economics and Finances of the Large Metropolis*

RAYMOND VERNON

I TAKE IT FOR granted that my fellow contributors employed in this joint exploration of the life of the metropolis look for the continued growth of giant urban clusters in this country, expanding in population at rates at least as fast as—perhaps faster than—the nation's total population growth. I assume too that there is very little disagreement on the general pattern of that growth. I envisage that the really big growth within these oversized metropolitan complexes will take place outside of the old cities which usually lie at the core of these clusters; that it will be primarily a suburban expansion, spreading thinly over the landscape and using up large quantities of land which not so long ago were cow pastures and cornfields. This general pattern of growth suggests that as a nation we are facing the exacerbation of some old problems, such as transportation, and some new ones as well. To get a more solid sense of what these problems are, however, one has to know a little more about the likely character of urban development.

GROWTH IN THE URBAN COMPLEX

No one needs to be told any longer that the great growth of population in the suburbs surrounding our crowded cities has been speeded by the passenger car and truck, coupled with rapidly rising living standards. Despite all the discussion about the richness of city living and the rewards of propinquity, most of us who are a part of the western culture want to have our cake and eat it too; we want to be near the city, not in it. And we seem willing to pay the price of suburban living, including the cost of transporting ourselves to and from the city in order to partake of its economic and cultural opportunities.

Some drift into the city after a taste of suburban life; their suburban neighbors have proved dull and intrusive, or their lawns have proved a malevolent tyrant. But all the available statistics, such as they are, suggest that this is distinctly a minority reaction, more typical of the intellectuals who write about the metropolis than of their fellows mortals. Most people who have any choice in the matter seem to take to the suburbs with a minimum of grousing, enjoying the security of living among their peers and the insulation from such untouchable city dwellers as Negroes, Mexicans, hillbillies, and Puerto Ricans.

Nor does the future demographic pattern suggest a very different set of preferences in the future for those who have a choice. Over the next two or three decades, there will be more growth at the two tail ends of the demographic curve than in the middle—the greatest growth will be among the very young and the rather old. There has been considerable wistful speculation that the increase among the aged will lay the basis for a revived city growth. The theory is, of course, that older people will find their suburban homes and their automobile-oriented travel patterns to be a heavy burden, and that they will react by moving to the city.

But it is chimerical to suppose that any such move could be the basis for a general city revival. For one thing, the numbers involved are not all that large. For another, the cost of capturing space near the part of the city that really matters—near the cultural and business centers—is prohibitively high and promises to remain so; just why, we shall make clear a bit later on. Finally, many in the older group have obvious alternatives to a return to the city and seem already to be exploiting those alternatives. One is to migrate to more pastoral settings. Now that the airplane makes travel fast and easy, and the decision to migrate does not involve the final separation from children and grandchildren, this would seem to be an attractive alternative for older people. The scraps of evidence we have been able to collect show a net exodus of older people out of metropolitan areas since 1940, and an even larger net exodus out of the central city portions of these areas. The other alternative for the aging suburban dweller is to give up his house for a suburban apartment located in the neighborhood where he has lived. This, at least, keeps him closer to the social structure which he knows and often keeps him closer to his grown children and grandchildren as well. For most, these are much more tangible advantages than those which city life has to offer.

True, some will return to the city, drawn back by the increasing difficulty of finding an "exclusive" suburb within tolerable commuting distance from a job in the city center. But these will be an elite group, able to pay for precious space close by the central district or for some strategic and attractive location a few minutes away by car. For this group, the endless neighborhoods of deteriorating middle-rent and low-rent housing which ring large city centers in a belt many miles deep would not be an acceptable alternative to the remote suburb.

The demographic future of the big cities inside our growing metropolitan areas is affected by still another force. The phenomenon of slum crowding is much more complex than some of its popular descriptions would allow—and by some measures, much less extensive. Slum crowding can be thought of as a phase in the growth cycle of an aging city neighborhood. Just before it appears, the neighborhood commonly is going through a period of population decline; the middle-income inhabitants of the slums-to-be are growing old, are being left behind by their grown-up children, and are finding their dwelling places increasingly unsuited for the washing machines, automobiles, and other possessions which a rising income and changing technology have made possible. Accordingly, their row houses and apartments grow ripe for downgrading and for higher densities. As the newest untrained outlanders appear in the city to join the labor force—green, ignorant of housing conditions, uncertain of their job future—they fill the downgraded properties, crowding them far beyond the densities for which they were designed. Because these newly arrived outlanders are usually quite young, they quickly add to their numbers with the arrival of children.

The history of the older portions of our big cities, however, indicates that this overcrowding phase eventually comes to an end. In a repetition of the middle-income cycle preceding it, the low-income family ages; the children and the boarders depart for newer neighborhoods; the seed couple often remains behind in the old, worn quarters, spreading out in some of the space which once they shared with children and boarders. Population declines, therefore, have come to be endemic in the older portions of most large American cities. Soon, this will be the dominant demographic characteristic of many such cities.

Enough about population trends for the moment. What about jobs? We have already implied two things about the distribution of jobs, two things which seem to run at cross purposes. In the first place, the automobile and the truck have extended the radius of the metropolitan area, not only for homes, but also for jobs. A grocery distributor no longer needs to be located alongside a river dock or at a rail head in order to receive his supplies; and he can distribute to retailers within a forty-mile radius rather than a five-mile radius if he chooses. On similar lines, a mill no longer need locate within walking distance of a trolley line in order to recruit its labor; it can count on workers' driving twenty or thirty miles to their jobs. So most manufacturing and distributing activities have taken advantage of the new-found freedom by spreading out on the land, exploiting all of the cost advantage of spacious sites. The result has been that manufacturing and distributing jobs have been falling off in the older portions of the old cities, while

growing at a rapid clip practically everywhere else in metropolitan areas, particularly in the open spaces.

There is a major slice of economic activity—several slices,
in fact—which have responded rather differently to their new-
found transportation freedom. Many of these have a need
which speedy transportation does not really satisfy; this is the
need for constant face-to-face communication with a variety
of other entities outside the firm. Elite decision makers of the
big central offices usually want to be near a complex of
lawyers, bankers, advertising agencies, accountants, and management advisers in order to tap their expertise on short notice.
Traders in the volatile money markets want to be near others
like them, continuously to swap rumors, ferret out information,
and provide mutual reassurance. Sellers of unstandardized
products want to be near one another to share the attention
of visiting buyers. And so on.

Groups such as these have preferred to remain tightly clustered in the central business districts of the old cities and to
grow there. If they have changed their locational preferences
at all, it has been a complex change. In some cases, enterprises
have reorganized themselves to retain the functions with
communication needs in the central business district while relocating the repetitive, routine, standardized functions elsewhere; the sales offices of the garment industries, for instance,
have clung to the city sales districts, while the sewing of the
garments has moved off. In other cases, offices located in the
central business district of one city have moved to the office
center of another city, as the growth of air travel or other considerations have changed the relative attractions of the competing cities.

The compulsion of activities of this sort has been to cluster
with related enterprises, in order to minimize communication
time and cost. It is true, therefore, that if clusters such as these
began to develop afresh today, no one could be sure exactly
where they would grow. But they began in the downtown portions of the old cities a century or more ago, pinned there by

such anachronistic factors as the location of the railroad termini and the limited supply of literate clerks. Once located, their very existence was a powerful lodestone for added growth.

These communication-oriented activities are a fast-growing part of the nation's economy. Their growth—at least their growth as measured by employment and space-occupying criteria—could be stunted, of course. Technological advances in office equipment will hold down office growth somewhat. And some really startling advances in the media of communication—something better and cheaper than closed-circuit television—might change the need for clustering and cause the establishments to scatter. But we are inclined to believe that the largest cities of the country will continue to see modest growth in these activities in their downtown areas.

What of the city areas outside of "downtown"? What of the remaining 90 per cent or so of big-city space which falls outside the central business districts—in residential neighborhoods, industrial enclaves, and the like? The neighborhoods that are strait-jacketed by street grids laid out for an earlier era and encumbered by obsolescent structures have little to offer the private industrial developer which he could not acquire more readily in spaces farther out. Accordingly, such neighborhoods are showing the signs of prospective loss. Some are already losing. Nor are trends of this sort limited to neighborhoods in the older central cities. They are beginning to appear in suburban cities as well, wherever the settlement pattern was already fixed in the pre-automobile age.

One way of summing up the story is this: the new suburbs of the giant metropolitan areas are growing fast and promise to continue their growth in population and jobs, using the land lavishly as they develop. The central business districts at the very core of the large metropolitan areas have elements of vitality which could have the effect of increasing—or at any rate upgrading—their jobs and their resident populations. In between the central business districts and the new suburbs,

however, the likely predominant pattern is one of a thinning
out and aging of the populations, a continued deterioration of
the physical plant, and a stagnation or decline of the job
market.

BALANCING INCOME WITH OUTGO

The pattern of change we envisage suggests various things
for the future of the old cities inside the urban mass. Holding
transportation and housing needs aside for the moment—we
shall discuss them later on—it seems evident that the current
problems will probably grow more acute.

It is true that, as the residents of these cities grow older and
as their numbers shrink, some of the cities' problems may ease
off. The cost of opening up new neighborhoods, including the
investment in streets, sewers, water mains, and schools, is unlikely to figure so prominently in future budgets. There will be
the renewal of existing plants to deal with, of course, but this
is a deferrable expense—deferrable in the sense that a failure
to renew is unlikely to generate the same kind of acute political
response among city voters that the total absence of a municipal facility might generate.

But as the shrinkage in city populations occurs, there may be
limits on the extent to which the cities can cut back on their
existing municipal facilities. If our prognosis is right, the population decline we foresee will be the result of a thinning-out
process, that is, a decline in the size of the average family
occupying a dwelling unit. We do not envisage the wholesale
abandonment of neighborhoods and the rapid rise of vacancies
in tenements and new houses. Instead, older people will
simply use more space per head.

This pattern of population decline means that there will be
obstacles in the way of reducing police or fire protection, clos-
ing off libraries or schools, shutting down water mains, or
blocking off streets. Here and there, such measures may be
possible. By and large, however, it may not be possible to re-

duce the facilities *pari passu* with the population they serve.

On top of this, as the city population ages, the proportion of the population which is unemployable or in poor health will probably rise a little; it may even be that the absolute number of such people, as well as the proportion, will rise. Accordingly, quite apart from the pressures produced by constantly rising professional and social standards in the welfare field, the demand for welfare services may go up in the old cities.

Pressures of this sort are hardly novel. The responses of the cities to these pressures have taken a number of forms. One, of course, has been to raise the real property tax rate or to stiffen assessment standards so that the tax yields could be increased. But the real property tax, as so many experts have observed, cannot be pushed forever upward. The tax is so brutally visible and hits the taxpayer with so direct an impact that any proposal for an increase almost automatically faces impassioned opposition. Besides, as the tax yields rise, problems of equity become more severe, and the city's fear of losing business to the suburbs grows apace. Accordingly, another response of the cities to the need for more revenue has been to impose new taxes in the form of sales and payroll levies.

This kind of response has made a good deal of sense, given the changing function of the old cities. As they have come to specialize in trade and office work and to lose ground in manufacturing, the amount of real property occupied by any enterprise has become a poorer index of its ability to pay. The shift from a real property tax to a levy on money flows such as a sales tax or a payroll tax, therefore, has probably established a somewhat closer correspondence between ability and liability among taxpayers in the cities.

Another factor probably supports the wisdom of the shift for the older cities. Good tax strategy demands that the city should avoid taxing economic entities which are in a position to respond by fleeing the jurisdiction; or to turn the proposition around, that the city concentrate its taxes on economic entities which have the least choice about remaining in the city. Of all

the various types of economic activity, manufacturing establishments with heavy real property commitments typically rank
among those with the weakest ties to the city; there are occasional exceptions, of course, such as newspaper plants and
bakeries, but by and large the generalization seems valid. At
the same time, wholesale and retail sales outlets appear to
have the least choice in finding an alternative location outside
the city. Once more, we must not overlook the seeming exceptions, such as department stores, but neither must we exagger-
ate the degree of locational choice of such outlets nor their
relatively minor importance as a proportion of the total sales
in most cities. We are inclined to suspect, therefore, that the
disposition of big cities will be to make more and more urgent
demands on state legislatures for the authority to impose sales
taxes and payroll taxes and that the use of such taxes by big
cities will increase with time.

The fiscal problems of the raw suburbs are quite different,
of course, from those of the central cities. From a septic-tank
and artesian-well civilization, sleepy semi-rural communities
on the edge of an urban mass have suddenly been projected
into the nightmare of financing water mains, sewage lines, new
schools, professional fire companies, and so on—and all in the
briefest span of time. Their problems in this regard have been
worse than that which the older cities had experienced in the
course of their growth. The older cities, by and large, covered
much more territory than the little new communities; hence,
while growth was occurring at the edges of the cities, there
were settled neighborhoods inside the city boundaries to help
finance their growth. Small suburban communities hit by the
growth tornado, however, encompass no such variety of neighborhoods; when they are overrun by progress, they are often
totally involved in the phenomenon.

These raw communities have other problems which make
their lot especially hard. Once they are hit by urban growth,
the facilities they are expected to provide are not the rough-
and-ready makeshifts with which cities could satisfy their con-

stituents half a century ago. All at once, they are expected to provide municipal facilities which are in accord with the expectations of an urban society in the mid-twentieth century. Worse still, they are expected to provide these urban facilities to a taxpaying group which persists in living in a dispersed pattern, 5,000 or so to the square mile instead of the 100,000 or so in the old cities. Roads, water mains, and fire-fighting apparatus must be provided to suit urban appetites in non-urban surroundings. Little wonder that the resulting fiscal needs are high.

But all the urban world is not divided simply between the old central cities and the new suburbs. There are two other sectors of the urban structure which need mentioning. One of these is the older suburban cities, like Camden, Evanston, and Newark. Demographically, many of these cities are going through a phase not unlike that of the central cities. Accordingly, the prospective fiscal problems of these older suburban cities bear many similarities to those of the central cities—but with some differences. The suburban cities have much less expectation of corralling and holding communication-oriented activities of the sort that cluster in the central cities; on the contrary, their competition for a place in the economic sun is principally with the shopping centers and highway stores of an automobile age, and their chance for success in the competition in general is quite low. As a result, unlike the central cities, these suburban cities dare not resort to such taxes as sales or payroll levies, except at the risk of driving out business. Even if they could impose such taxes with impunity, most of them are not large enough to administer these kinds of taxes with the sophisticated expertise that they demand.

We must not leave the impression, however, that the whole of the urban world is in desperate fiscal straits. For there is another sector still—our fourth and final one—which is suffering no particular fiscal pain. In most large metropolitan areas, we find a comparatively large group of mature, well-established suburban communities, growing moderately if at all, well equipped with schools and other municipal facilities, well able to meet their fiscal obligations. We hear little from this group, except for some occasional grousing as the tax rate goes up to match municipal salary increases. But the grousing is usually subdued, since in general the tax increases in communities of this sort probably have not been as large as the income growth of their inhabitants. Despite the comparatively unsung existence of this sector, there are indications that it is a not inconsiderable proportion of the larger metropolitan community.

It is not hard to foresee the nature of the tax struggle that is shaping up. By one device or another, the hard-pressed cities and raw suburban towns will be looking for ways to tap the tax resources of their comparatively prosperous neighbors. The devices will vary as they have in the past, depending in part on pure chance, local custom, and local law. But two popular devices will surely be used in increasing degree: the use of the special district, set up to merge the school system or other municipal service of hard-pressed areas with those of their less pressured neighbors; and the use of higher state taxes and larger state subsidies to localities, granted in support of some specific service. These devices may well miscarry at times, especially the state subsidy technique. That is to say, the system may in the end provide the largest subsidies to these areas that seem to need them least, as the interests of the rural areas and the well-to-do communities of the state struggle with those of the hard-pressed cities and raw suburbs over the division of the spoils. But more resort to the state approach seems altogether likely.

One is tempted at times to remove the lead weights of reality from his earthbound feet and to ask what other solution for local fiscal problems might be conceived. The obvious one, apart from leveling the differences in tax burdens and services through state-aid and special-district devices, is to create a new level of general government at the metropolitan level, with powers to tax and spend supplementary to or in lieu of the localities below. Pioneer efforts of this sort in the United States have run up against stony resistance. Whatever the expert may think of the desperate need for innovation in government, the failures of existing government are not so obvious, as seen through the eyes of the average urban dweller, as to justify major surgery. Besides, moves of this sort are conceived to fly in the face of the American tradition of local self-government; they raise specters for the well-placed communities of public services dragged down to mediocre levels; and so on. We see little future for this approach. But some of what it would accomplish will be achieved less obviously by other means.

RAILS AND RUBBER

Our picture of the future development of the metropolis, if it should come to pass, carries with it some fairly explicit implications about the future of passenger transportation within the great metropolitan areas of the country.

No one needs to be told that the problem of moving people daily from their homes to their jobs constitutes one of the major headaches of many metropolitan areas. There are two distinguishable kinds of problems. One is that of physical facilities: though the number of jobs in central cities seems hardly to be growing, nevertheless the roads, bridges, tunnels, and parking areas—even the suburban trains and subway facilities—simply seem too limited for the traffic that they carry. The other is a problem of finances: though the mass transit suburban trains and subways seem well filled, somehow the companies that own them seem constantly on the verge of bankruptcy. These are some provoking paradoxes that demand understanding.

The reasons for the overburdening of the roads, highways, and parking areas are the most transparent part of the puzzle. As people have dispersed outward on the land, far from the suburban railway stations and the city subways, the relative attractiveness of commuting by automobile has grown. The first stage of the commuting journey, in any case, has demanded the use of a car; and once ensconced behind a wheel, one often thinks it sensible to make the whole journey by car. The propensity for car travel has been increased, of course, by the rise in car ownership—an inevitable concomitant of dispersed suburban living.

Another trend—a less obvious trend on the whole—has added to the peak flows of traffic between suburb and central city. This is the rise of "reverse commuting," that is, the increased use of daily car pools bearing the lower-income residents of the central cities outward to their jobs in warehouses, factories, and retail stores dispersed through the suburban areas. Here, too, the need to make the final leg of the journey by some form of automotive conveyance or on foot has often prodded the commuter into making the whole trip by automobile.

All this increased hauling of wage earners across the face of the metropolis, it should be noted, would take place even without any assumption about job increases in the central city. The dispersal of medium-income and high-income families from the city center and the dispersal of low-income jobs from the center are all that is needed to generate the increased flows.

While the suburban rail facilities have been losing some of their customers to the highways, at the same time they have been gaining others. The outward trek of homes from the central cities has carried many commuters outside of the range of central city trolley, subway, and bus systems into the orbit of the suburban rails. Most of the rails, therefore, have not lacked for rush-hour business.

What they have lost is the off-hour and week-end trade. The suburban housewife who takes the 10:45 into the central city for a day of shopping downtown and the suburban couple who take the 7:32 for an evening at the theater are a vanishing species. Off-hour and week-end traffic are now almost entirely in the province of the highway. For the railroads, this has been a cruel blow. Off-peak business had been the bread and butter of the rail system, since it could be accommodated without added manpower or equipment. The principal business left to the rails, therefore—the peak-hour business—has been of the kind which is least profitable.

At the same time, the suburban railroads have had other problems. Featherbedding practices plus pervasive government regulation have rocked these institutions into a state of technological moribundity. Few rail systems have had the will or the means to meet the challenge of changing transportation needs. The possibilities of pruning labor costs through mechanization have barely been scratched, partly because the rails have been unsure whether the unions would tolerate the necessary changes. The possibilities of devising coordinated mass transit systems which could capture some of the reverse commuting business or could serve the needs of commuters traveling circumferentially between different suburbs have also been neglected. If such innovations could be developed on paper, as they no doubt can, there is still the problem of obtaining the needed governmental action and the problem of gaining approval for a system of rates which would return the investment. Facing such problems, the long-run strategy of many suburban railroads has been to pull out of the passenger business as rapidly as possible.

The problems of subways and surface cars in the big cities have been of a somewhat different sort. Few of these systems have increased their business in recent years, as measured by paid trips; many have actually been losing ground by such a yardstick. In New York City, for instance, the decline has been in evidence for several decades. Once again, however, the lucrative off-peak business has fallen off faster than the rush-hour traffic. To add to the difficulties of these systems, the business that remains has consisted more and more of long-haul trips between the edges of the city and the very center, a fact which puts a particularly heavy strain on any system with a flat fare. Finally, the business at some termini in the central city—those located in the office district—has grown in some cases as the central city's jobs have tended to become more and more specialized in office work. To those using the subway system, therefore, the facilities sometimes seem progressively overcrowded and inadequate, even though the system as a whole may be operating well under capacity.

One line of remedial action suggested with increasing frequency by city planners has been to alter the relative prices of transportation services. It has been assumed that if somehow the use of the automobile could be made more expensive relative to the rail, this might check the shift from rail to rubber. To achieve this result, a variety of proposals have been made. One approach has been to introduce or increase public subsidies for mass transit facilities. Another has been to raise the tolls on bridges and tunnels and increase the fees on central city parking. Various difficulties have hobbled these approaches, however.

Where subsidies were proposed, the first hurdle—not the only one, by any means—has been the problem of finding the money. Where raising the cost to the motorist has been proposed, it has evoked the fear that prospective commuters to the central city might respond, not by turning back to the use of the rail, but by avoiding the central city altogether. The response of some shoppers could well be to shop more in the suburbs and less in the central city. And other kinds of business might be lost to the central city as well.

Another difficulty is one which has arisen out of the institutional structure of the entities operating the subways, railroads, bridges, tunnels, and parking areas. In many metropolitan areas, the ownership of these competing or complementary facilities is vested in a maze of public and private bodies. The suburban railroads ordinarily are privately owned, though subject to federal, state, and local regulations. The subways, surface lines, and buses are sometimes private, sometimes public; when public they are sometimes run by a division of general government, sometimes by an independent authority. The tunnels and bridges are almost invariably public, usually under the control of a separate authority and insulated from the influence which the electorate might bring to bear. The notion of coordinating these systems has rarely been explicitly considered. Where it has, however, one obvious problem has arisen at once: those entities that are solvent want to avoid entangling alliances with those that are not. In some areas, this has meant that agencies which purvey services to the motorist are careful to steer clear of those responsible for the operation of mass transit facilities. What is more, their desire to do so is often supported by a public conviction that somehow this separation is "sound business."

The difficulties do not end here, however. Still another obstacle to a coordinated metropolitan transport policy derives from the fact that the central city and the suburban cities and towns see themselves—quite rightly—as rivals in the great game of attracting business and taxes. One may say that this is a short-sighted view—that the deterioration of a metropolitan area's means of internal circulation will eventually damage all its parts. But, unhappily, it is also true that the *improvement* of a metropolitan area's means of internal circulation may damage some of its parts as well. And where some area sees itself as the prospective victim of a metropolitan improvement, one can hardly expect it to participate in the change without demur. So it is that we find some suburban cities, wisely or otherwise, resisting the development of highways which bypass their downtown shopping districts.

There is no doubt that comprehensive regional approaches to the transportation problem could provide better transportation than the existing fragmented system. The facilities for commuter travel are so closely complementary that their pooled use opens up vistas now excluded by organizational and political boundaries. In some measure, such approaches will probably develop. It may not be difficult, for instance, to pool a number of rail lines in different jurisdictions if all of

them are losing money. But the pooling of vehicular facilities
with rail facilities will prove a harder nut to crack. Here, the
built-in jurisdictional hurdles seem so high as to be nearly
insurmountable.

What we envisage, therefore, is primarily a series of pallia-
tives within the mass transit field. Some states show signs of
getting into the problem, for instance, by providing help in
meeting the capital needs of the mass transit facilities and by
enacting measures to encourage local tax abatement for such
facilities. It is not farfetched to suppose that the federal government will eventually get into mass transit as well, sucked
in as an inexorable consequence of its present involvement in
the financing and planning of the nation's highway system.
One way or another, there will be efforts to redress the balance
between mass transit and the automobile. But the results
promise to be slow in coming and fragmentary in their application. In fact, before such results materialize, the most pressing
transportation problem inside some metropolitan areas may
have changed in character. Instead of wondering how to haul
people to and from the central business district with comfort
and dispatch, our prime question may well be how to move
people from the dispersed homes in one suburb to the dispersed plants in another.

OBSOLESCENCE AND DECAY

According to our argument, the private demand for space in
the central business districts of the old cities may well continue
fairly strong. But the private demand for space in the grey
areas beyond seems weak. Here populations promise to thin
out; retail trade will decline; factory jobs should stabilize or
fall off in number; and no private force seems at hand with
sufficient incentive to recapture such space for other uses.

The central cities and the old suburban communities are
unlikely to sit by, however, as they see the populations in their
grey areas decline and the streets and structures grow old and

outdated. They will try to arrest the rot as they have been trying in the past. And they will succeed in some measure, just as they have in the past. All told, these efforts at rejuvenation —many of them the efforts of private civic bodies rather than exclusively those of governments—have had a visible impact.

While acknowledging the impact of these efforts and the truly heroic contributions of some groups and individuals in bringing them about, however, one must also soberly recognize their limitations and appraise their future scope.

These efforts have produced their most spectacular successes in or near the central business districts of the old cities. This means two things: first, the impact of these successes upon our collective consciousness has been many times larger than the areas involved—many times larger than the impression we would glean as we observed the total urban mass from a helicopter, for instance. Second, the efforts at rehabilitation have been made precisely in those sections of the city where, as we indicated earlier, a real private demand for space has existed; these civic and governmental efforts have been floating with the currents of the private real estate market, not bucking them.

Every technique so far devised for recapturing the obsolete portions of old cities where no such private demand exists has been breathtakingly costly to the public purse. The cost of recapturing an acre of old buildings in the built-up grey areas of old cities of our metropolitan areas commonly runs over $500,000, though old suburban cities have sometimes been known to recapture such sites at a price as low as $100,000. Once the expenditure is made, all that society has is a leveled site. A new suburban site suitably supplied with roads and utilities and close enough for most purposes to an urban center usually can be had for $15,000 or $25,000 an acre. At a cost of, say, $160,000,000 per square mile, we are bound soberly to ask how many square miles of rotted urban streets and structures the public authorities are likely to raze.

The bulldozer is not the only means for reconverting an

urban environment, however. There is always the possibility
of urban renewal of other sorts. Old structures are sometimes
sound enough to invite rebuilding; and if the rebuilding takes
place all at once in an entire neighborhood, one sees hope of
giving the neighborhood as a whole a new lease on life. But
at what cost? Here again, the facts are a little disconcerting.
The cost of remodeling, rewiring, replastering and repainting
"sound" old city structures, according to some pilot projects,
comes to about $3,000 per room—about as much as building
a room from scratch in a modest one-family house in the suburbs. Add the cost of acquiring the city structure, and what
we have is high-cost housing, not housing for middle- and
low-income groups.

Cost considerations aside, however, there is another reason
to doubt that urban renewal will take the form of a vast subsidized bulldozing and rebuilding of cities in new dwelling
units for medium-income and low-income families. As far as
middle-income families are concerned, there is nothing in our
analysis to support the notion that their demand for suitable
housing in the grey areas is really very large; certainly, the
prospective location of jobs in metropolitan areas and the
present and prospective structure of social values in American
life offer no promise on this score. And as for low-income
families, if our analysis is right, their demand for dwelling
units in the grey areas may actually decline. The families dependent on the relatively low-income jobs in retail trade and
consumer services, in goods handling, and in unskilled factory
operations will find declining opportunities in the city and increasing ones outside; their disposition will be—indeed, it
already is—to follow the jobs by finding quarters in the older
sections of suburban cities, even if this requires the overcrowding of such quarters.

Two *caveats* to these sweeping propositions must be made at
once. One is the observation that a ready market does exist at
this very moment for a considerable added amount of subsidized low-rent or medium-rent housing in the grey areas of

many of our central cities. But we would guess that the size of this unsatisfied demand, at least for housing located in the grey areas well removed from the central business district, is not expanding but shrinking. Our second qualification has to do with the inevitability of the shrinkage. Symbols such as the home in the suburb can probably be changed by massive psychic and physical intervention. A giant garden city in the middle Bronx—so vast as to constitute a new neighborhood socially segregated from the denizens of the obsolescent structures about it—might conceivably find takers, especially if it were being reproduced with suitable fanfare many times over throughout America. But the intervention would have to be much larger in scope and far fresher in concept than anything so far seriously proposed.

It is safer to assume that the pattern of urban renewal will be shaped by events more than it will shape those events. In the great central cities, the thinning out of populations in the grey areas will create the possibility of recapturing some open space, and this will no doubt be done. The old suburban cities may find more need for added low-cost public housing than the central cities. But their ability to convert that need into an operating public program may not be as great as the central cities', simply because the size of a suburban city is sometimes not sufficient to allow it to acquire the skilled technical staff needed to plan and carry out such programs. It may be that, at this stage, the state and federal governments will assume more direct responsibility for such programs simply in order to fill the breach, or that regional authorities will be created to handle the housing problem for groups of municipalities. One way or another, the suburban cities may fill a part of their needs, but the institutional problem will be a very real one.

Of course, if urban land were to prove an acutely scarce resource at some point in the future, this picture might be very different. Then, the pressure to recapture the "underused" grey areas for living space might be so strong as to generate vast expenditures to that end. But it is one of the paradoxes of urban growth today that the increase in the supply of urban land is probably outstripping the demand. At the edges of most urban masses, farmers are shrinking their land use, on the whole, faster than developers are taking the land up. Part of the reason for this shrinkage is that farmers have been unwilling or unable to match the wage structure of the nearby urban labor market and have been encountering increasing difficulties in holding onto their hired hands. Part of it has been due to the swiftly increasing productivity of agriculture coupled with a relatively stable output. As a result, as geographers are pointing out, the amount of acreage covered with scrub forest on the edges of the great urban masses on the Eastern seaboard has been increasing in recent years, not shrinking. The deer are reappearing in large numbers, to nibble voraciously at the tender foundation plantings of the anxious suburbanite.

Eventually, of course, this will change. Urban land will become scarce again as sheer population growth fills up the empty spaces. But the land promises to grow more plentiful before it grows scarce again. And for several decades, we are likely to see suburban developments making more and more profligate use of the land.

THE TOTAL PATTERN

What we foresee, on the whole, is a pattern of continued change in the large metropolitan complex not vastly different from the change recently in evidence. That we should have come to this general conclusion was perhaps inevitable. Man's favorite technique of projection has always been to extrapolate the recent past.

Seen from the viewpoint of the people who live in this urban setting of the future, the problems may not seem much more severe than they do today; indeed, some problems may seem to have been mitigated. The housing conditions of the low-income groups, if our prognosis is right, may seem no worse and may even appear to have been alleviated a little. The problem of hauling people to the central city and back will not grow so swiftly as inevitably to outrun the countermoves of the Robert Moseses of the urban world.

Still, the continued change will flush up incipient problems and exacerbate old ones to the point at which they may appear as new questions. The continued decline in the population of the old neighborhoods may appear as a fresh problem as it begins to reduce the total population of old cities. The growing financial problems of the old cities and the mass transit systems may acquire the crisis label very soon, as well.

Crises commonly engender unpredictable reactions. As earth-bound mortals, however, we have been bound to stress only what is predictable. On that basis, we see measures at the margin which will ease the problems to the point at which they are barely tolerable but not measures which will greatly change their character. It is on this score that the blinders with which all mortals are equipped may prove to have betrayed us.

4. The Influence of Technology on Urban Forms

AARON FLEISHER

THE IDEA THAT there exists in technology a potential capable of radically modifying the conditions of human existence has made prophecy a matter for common concern. In former times, when life and death were the only great changes noticeable or conceivable, the future was a drama to be played in the next world. Prediction, accordingly, was the proper function of priests. In this world only the roles and the lines remained; the players were anonymous and the sets indifferent.

The sense of time quickened, however, when change became documented. A new mode of travel, a new means of communication or source of power made the shape of the immediate future a cause for debate equally in commerce and philosophy. But these recent prophets were usually more concerned with the effects of technology on the particulars of their own interests. A synoptic view was rare, even until the immediate present. J. B. S. Haldane's *Dædalus, or the Science of the Future* and Bertrand Russell's *Icarus, or the Future of Science* were isolated examples.

To realize the larger view, however, is hardly a simple matter. One has to anticipate the potentialities of technology, as well as the course of all the other changes that flow independently from technology, then gauge the interaction of both kinds of change—which compounds the problem of prediction at least thrice. These compound predictions can be considered an example of what is called systems analysis. I suspect, however, that the kinship between such analysis and these compound predictions is too remote for much help. But it is a comfort to know that one is not alone.

The utopians should have contributed something to this problem, for, being concerned only with an ideal society and not with the historical process, they could bypass the more difficult part of the prediction and deal only with the interactions. But they ignored these, thinking it unnecessary to question the consistency of the society described and the technology prescribed. An organization tailored to a people who travel by dogcart and communicate by radio need not also fit one who travel by airplane and communicate by smoke signals. The omission is not a trivial one, even when the society is fully synthesized and then set in motion. Not every static society is a stable one. An important test of a utopian proposal, one that is rarely run, is its stability in the presence of perturbations.

To separate the influences technology will have on the city is an example of such a compounded problem in prediction. An estimate of the future of technology is a difficult but not an unreasonable question, certainly somewhat safer now than fifty years ago. We know more now, therefore the possibilities are easier to assess, and the present concern with limits (limits of devices, of principles, and even of knowledge) adumbrates an upper boundary to conjecture.

The city is a large, complex, loose-linked organization. Its equipment is bulky, immobile, costly, and obsolesces at a rate that is rarely faster than decades. Sometimes, the rate of obsolescence is even negative, since some equipment becomes more valuable with the passage of time. By contrast, research is no longer exotic, and its pace has become so quick that the distinction between science and engineering is difficult to maintain. The flows of urban and technological time, therefore, are not commensurate. In how many cities are the streets so arranged as to delight the motorist? And when they are modified, the expense is huge, the pain intense, and the conversion a compromise. Whatever the reason for the lag between these two kinds of time, it does exist, and therefore fifty years of urban history is at most equivalent to thirty years of technology.

This fact represents a dislocation in time. There is perhaps another dislocation in value. The gap between the capability and the usable product is an expensive one. Even if the economy were rich enough, the society might not choose to pay the cost of development. And when resources are finite, proper allocation requires some measure of desire and advantage. I prefer to avoid such market analyses, for they are enmeshed in matters of taste and policy.

By urban form I mean only the density of population as a function of locus in the city, and the time of day. Such a definition ignores some kinds of experience entirely and treats many others lightly; but it does capture an important characteristic of the use of land, and it contains, at least by implication, some of the operational and structural constraints on the city. Moreover, to specify urban patterns in greater detail than future changes in technology can be anticipated would be a wasteful mismatch. Time is a dimension we have hardly mastered, and modesty, therefore, requires that all but the largest changes be smoothed.

This definition of urban form provides a rationale for sorting technology by relevance. New foods and clothing, for example, are irrelevant. New products and materials, as a general category, are irrelevant. New industries, except in their locational eccentricities, are irrelevant. None of these is likely to modify the spacing of people.

At the other end of the scale of relevance are the possible devices that will replace or separate people, or move them and their products. These devices span distance and time, and therefore changes in transportation and communication are especially relevant. An inquiry into the manner in which technology affects urban forms might profitably be pursued by raising these specific questions. Are there any physical limits to growth? Will changes in communications and transportation favor any particular pattern of density? To what degree will the response depend on size and geography?

THE LIMIT ON SIZE

Some simple rules of thumb taken from demography suggest that toward the middle of the next fifty-year period a city of twenty-five million can exist. Such a concentration would be unworkable if either external supply or internal distribution should prove too expensive. There is almost no possibility of an absolute failure. I assume that the entire population of the country will always be adequately supported. If there are no national shortages, then the external supply is a problem of import, and therefore of total channel capacities: port, rail, truck, and air. About five times New York's capacity is a reasonable estimate, and this looks easily attainable from the present capabilities of the large seaport cities, without any substantial increase in the unit cost. However, supply will not have to depend on present means. Capacity will increase as pipelines and airlines move more deeply into the freight business, and channels will be used more intensively as cargo juggling becomes easier.

As for supplying the city itself, there is enough food now to support the larger population, at least in this country. But the industrial and domestic uses of electricity per person have hardly reached the saturation point. The amount of power required, therefore, will not increase simply as the number of people. Still, hydroelectric sources are not capable of indefinite extension. However large it may be, the amount of water in the atmosphere and on the earth's surface is finite. Whenever and wherever necessary, nuclear reactors can be used as supplementary sources, and these are likely to be used, as are conventional fuels, in thermal engines. Water, then, is a necessary component in the power-conversion cycle. Efficiency in its use is increasing, and the quality of the water need not be high. Location, therefore, will not be particularly critical, and where it is so, the capabilities for transmitting electricity will probably be equal to supplying urban centers from distant sources.

The amount of wastes that will accumulate will be monstrous, but by some chemical means they will be manageable. Radioactive waste, however, cannot be disposed of so lightly, and while the problem will not become critical within the next fifty years, if and when it does, the issues will be much more involved than the continued growth of cities.

The atmosphere is also used as a sewer. To judge from the intensity of the present concern with this problem and from the current rate of clearing, I would think that the noxious output per person will be cut at least by the amount of the increase in the population. If these new people did not spread at all, then the urban atmosphere would be no more loaded than it is today. Any pattern of lower density would improve matters. However, no account has been taken of local geography and climatology. Los Angeles, for example, is unfortunate in both these respects. Some comfort can be gathered from the prospect that the meteorologist will in the future be able to prescribe the optimum distributions for fixed sources of pollution. The automobile will require a different tactic.

An adequate water supply will not be easily assured. It should be possible to collect more water from a wider area, store it with less loss in larger dams, and transport it more efficiently to greater distances. The need for water, however, will increase faster than the population will. In time, then, a time which may occur within the next fifty years, new sources will be required. The sea is one such possible source; the control of rainfall is not likely to add very much. The location of new sources will usually be critical, and therefore transportation costs will be important. There is not very much new that can be done with aqueducts, and it is difficult to concentrate water. It will be expensive, and in some areas its lack may deter growth.

By the end of the fifty-year period the city may number fifty million. (The linear extrapolation is far less in error than the initial value of twenty-five million.) A factor of two, in my opinion, will have no marked effect on the external supply. What of the internal distribution? The price of things includes the cost of distribution. When all other circumstances remain the same, a difference in price becomes a clue to difficulties in distribution. Within the metropolis prices are fairly uniform and independent of density, and between cities there are only small differences. One can guess, then, that the cost of internal distribution does not vary across a wide range of densities, and that density would have to be rather larger than the largest value now known before one need worry about distribution.

THE EFFECTS OF CHANGES IN COMMUNICATIONS

Some description of the observed patterns of density is now in order. Most modern cities display a distribution of density of population that has a sharp maximum in one or several small central areas devoted largely to business, and a diffuse minimum, pock-marked with commerce, where people live. I take this to represent a real conviction, not a convenient compromise. In the mean, people choose to conduct their business in an environment that offers the greatest possible number of personal encounters and to spread their family affairs over as much space as they can afford. We need not here account for this choice; it is certainly not the only possible pattern of living, perhaps not the best or even the most efficient. Given this fact, how will it be modified by changes in communication?

The larger purpose of present research in communications is to design systems capable of transmitting information with greater degrees of reliability, fidelity, capacity, economy, and distance. Wherever the density is high, which is to say where personal encounters are important, fidelity is particularly relevant. Short of transmitting the actual person, the next most faithful representation is his picture. Let us suppose this kind of transmission to be as common as the telephone is today and not much more expensive.

One could easily compute the many occasions when the television screen would be a satisfactory replacement for the person himself. If these were advantages they would be relative. Where the replacement fails, however, the failure is absolute and therefore critical. What would be the legal status of a video presence? Would the courts recognize it? The salesman and the buyer might be unhappy with a picture, especially if their sources of information were also tactile or olfactory. Not that smell and feel are impossible to code and transmit; but the working solution will require time and money. Color transmission is easier, but it is still poor.

Are drawings to be examined? Can equipment be demonstrated by television? The surgeon cannot use it. Can the psychiatrist? How well can a multicornered conference be served? It may not be adequate for transactions that would terminate in a handshake—or a fist fight. Clearly, it would not suffice for encounters that culminate in an embrace. I do not know in how many contexts people and things are replaceable by pictures. Some are matters of taste and fashion, and perhaps the largest number of such substitutions will derive from this category. Yet even if these were many, the advantage to the entrepreneur might be ambiguous. He could argue that, having to meet with people at some time in his negotiations, he might well settle near them now and enjoy the advantages of both propinquity and television. The shift may be worth the cost of congestion.

The telephone was also a dramatic technological change and provides an enlightening parallel. It is a rather low-fidelity device, having about one one-thousandth of television bandwidth. But there are still personal encounters it could replace. Instead, the net result seems to have been an occasion to increase density. Having acquired an efficient means for preliminary negotiations and routine instructions, many people, ordinarily on the move, remained fixed. Space was saved and higher densities made workable. Television may have the same effect. By itself, it is ambivalent with respect to density.

Pocket-size portable transmitters and receivers are already available. These are low-fidelity, short-range devices—in effect, personal telephones—useful only where the density is high, which they would tend to increase. Communication devices do span distance, but that distance may be fairly small. They are not therefore technically trivial nor are their services unimportant. A seat in the gallery plus a pair of opera glasses is not as good as a box, but it is tolerable; and the man who takes a portable radio to the bleachers is not silly. All these are also examples of congestion ameliorated without diluting density.

For the woman of the house, the television screen may replace several shopping trips—certainly for standard items—and thus become the new mail-order catalog. (But if the package is standard I do not see why the telephone would not do as well.) The importance of the supermarket might then be reduced. Her children may be able to attend school by way of the television screen—but I doubt that she would consider it an advantage. The number of shopping trips to the central city is not likely to be affected. Neither Bonwit Teller nor Filene's basement can be surveyed by television.

The telephone has contributed to the exodus to the suburbs, but by itself it would have been powerless. A parallel means of transportation has to be available. With similar reservations, television might exert a similar influence. However, I doubt that it can be as effective. The difference the telephone created is very much larger than the added advantage of a television channel.

THE EFFECTS OF CHANGES IN OCCUPATIONS

Twice a day on most days the city experiences a wave of density created by people traveling to and from work. Therefore, it is in order to inquire into what changes can occur in the future in the distribution of occupations.

I think that we shall see automation increasing at almost all
levels of activity. People have long since ceased being significant sources of power. They are now being displaced as sources
of perception and judgment as well. We are acquainted with
the automatic oil refinery. There may be very few processes of
production that are exempt from an equivalent control. Nor
do the possibilities stop with production. Machines now exist
that are capable of assuming many clerical functions, admitting and filling orders, retrieving and filing information,
keeping records and accounts. They are also capable of a large
number of managerial functions, such as scheduling and controlling production, keeping and maintaining inventory, collect-
ing and routing shipments. To some degree they are capable
of replacing engineering and technical skills. How far into the
realm of policy-making these machines can penetrate is difficult
to decide. For present purposes, however, the ultimate limit is
not very important. The machine has demonstrated its ability
to affect a substantial part of the working population.

Changes in the complexion of occupations will depend on
the money available and the comparative advantages of the
machines: neither pick nor shovel is entirely obsolete. By the
end of the fifty-year period there may be a marked displacement of white- and blue-collar workers, certainly in the large
firms and to a lesser extent in government. The machines will
generate new occupations and increase the number of people
in others—but they are also susceptible to automatic processes
in their manufacture and, even more so, in their use and repair.
In time, the balance may show a net loss in jobs, more probably
in the central city; but the loss should not be very large. Many
firms in the city will not be affected, because their operations,
however varying, remain either too small or too specialized.

In another respect, the machines may provide occasions for
an increase in density. Now that growth, accretion, and di-
versification have become almost necessary for existence, a
good part of the business world has become a highly branched
affair. Many decisions that are being made locally and individually will, because of the advantages conferred by ma-

chines, be made centrally and collectively. A convergence of the intermediate layers of administration and control within the city is therefore to be expected; but how this will modify the pattern of density is less clear. The decision to locate, which is now based on minimizing some combination of cost and inconvenience in travel and communications, will probably be sufficient only to distinguish one metropolitan region from another. With respect to these rationalizations, the metropolis is fairly undifferentiated, for it is not by its facilities for travel and communication that its parts are best distinguished. In the future these facilities may be manipulated to influence a particular pattern of change, but such manipulations will not be matters of technology.

The requirements of the machine itself contribute very little to the locational decision. The information on which it feeds can arrive almost as well by wire as by person. A communication node is thereby required, but it need not coincide with a maximum in density of population. When management does centralize, it will probably favor the core of a large city, but its reasons for doing so will be neither economically nor technologically compelling.

Computers will probably tend to displace people in the core of all cities. In large cities they will make for a concentration of business controls and, therefore, of people. In such cities, the net change may not be a substantial one. There are kinds of counterflows in which the smaller cities can also participate. Local production and management may be attracted by the probability of a decrease in the price of newly vacated space, together with the fewer people and less parking space required per plant. At first glance, automated industries, being less dependent on labor, would appear to be freer to locate at will, but by themselves their working force may be insufficient to form a community. The town that is dependent on one or two industries will probably be rare. I should guess that, parallel to the recent migration from farm to city, there will be a movement from small to large cities.

The greatest effect the machine may have on cities is an

indirect one. The human work load will be substantially decreased. To provide for the new leisure can become a proper part of public policy, and therefore a substantial determinant of the form of the metropolis. The prospect is hardly novel. When Herbert Hoover spoke of a car in every garage, he was not thinking of the trip to work.

THE EFFECT OF CHANGES IN TRANSPORTATION

These will be sorted by scales of distance. Let us take in turn the central city, the metropolitan area, and a region of cities. The events in each scale are not independent, and are therefore not cumulative; these scales are devices of convenience. Consider the last one first. The complex of American cities—their locations, their functions, and their sizes—was determined in part by the transportation facilities of the nineteenth century, the railroads and waterways. A new means of transport that is sufficiently good can modify this complex by altering function and influencing relative rates of growth. The airplane may be one such means. For this purpose trucks are not essentially different from railroads. Therefore, the future balance between air and ground transport is relevant.

I do not think that any aspect of surface transportation—speed, efficiency, cost, or convenience—can improve by more than a factor of two; the wheel was a wonderful invention that reached the height of its development around the first half of the twentieth century. There is now being developed a kind of vehicle (the British call it a hovercraft) that rides on a layer of compressed air a very short distance above a surface. The surface need not be particularly smooth, and water serves very well. This vehicle has the obvious advantages of requiring only a cheap roadway and, compared to other surface vehicles, of generating a smaller amount of friction.

Over a long haul, these conveyances look capable of the loads and efficiencies of large trucks, with somewhat greater speeds. At best, they appear to promise no advantage where the network of roads is dense and the traffic heavy. Within the metropolis, their principle may be applicable to mass transit, but the possibility is a rather faint one. I do not count these vehicles as effective influences on future patterns of density.

The capabilities of the airplane place it in another class. It has already cut out a large portion of passenger transport and is now moving into hauling heavy freight. An aircraft that can take off and land vertically and fly at nearly three times the speed of sound is not an unreasonable projection. The national economy may then come under the influence of a new scale of time and distance. The nearest big city, the nearest shipping node, the nearest supply center can be five times farther than now. A new allocation of purpose and place with respect to transportation may develop. The larger cities will profit more, but the effect of their location is more difficult to decide.

What will the metropolitan scale of travel be in time and distance? If a region is to be considered a metropolis, travel should be possible between any two points with some reasonable daily facility. I take "reasonable" as requiring standards of comfort, scheduling, and time en route at least as good as those now available. If fifty million people are distributed in a metropolis with the average density of population of New York City today, they will cover an area equivalent to a circle twenty-five miles in radius; the density of Los Angeles would give a radius of sixty miles. Since the outlines of the city are not circular, these distances are at least half as short as they might be. Surface transportation under the best of circumstances will require several hours to get some people to work. To keep travel time within two hours, the average speed would have to be at least doubled. This means that each vehicle, whether automobile, bus, or train, must have its own right of way as well as some form of automatic safety controls. These requisites are feasible but expensive. If commuting is to be restricted to surface vehicles, then, in the sense of an easy interchange of people, the metropolis will be limited in extent. I have mentioned only the journey to and from work; the time allowed for others may be longer.

Aircraft engineers believe that in time they can provide a system of mass transit with a cruising speed of two hundred miles an hour, at a cost near that of the present systems. As with other mass-transit systems, the critical parameter is the mass. If such a system works at all, we may again see cities growing radially.

An alternate possibility is the one-car, one-airplane family. Aside from the parking problem, this seems possible. Since the private airplane must grow up within the federal airway system, it will probably acquire a strong sense of discipline from the beginning. Planners will therefore have an advantage with the private airplane that they have not yet acquired with the automobile. Even if the numbers of such aircraft are modest, the traffic problem will be formidable, for it will require keeping tabs on the origin, location, and destination of all flights over the metropolitan area. Airway channels can be as expensive and as offensive as the highways.

Patterns of density may be possible for an urban population of fifty million which are quite satisfactory and do not require the mobility that aircraft would add. In its most modest role, the airplane would supplement the surface system required by the enlarged city. That is how the automobile got started, but it was only because policy provided the roads that it could eventually determine the prevailing patterns of density. The airplane has somewhat the same potential, but the dangers are not quite similar. It is more expensive and more difficult to operate; it starts from a position of control; and we are no longer as innocent as we were when the automobile was young. This time we are likely to make different mistakes. That some form of aircraft may be a common vehicle neither commits nor limits patterns of density but rather increases the possible modes of changes and growth.

Technology is not likely to contribute very much to the solution of the problem caused by the crowding of people and vehicles in the city. Congestion does not behave like a simple symptom of malfunction; otherwise, its reduction would be largely a matter of adding capacity. A new road is the standard solution, but in fact it is often invalid because the subsequent traffic becomes even more intense. To blame the new imbalance on the growth of the city or on a redistribution of travel is a tacit admission that the channels are not passive participants in determining how the traffic will be shared. Therefore, congestion cannot be controlled by simple additions to the network of roads. In this respect, the network of highways resembles a system with destabilizing feedbacks.

Suppose nothing is done about congestion. I do not think people will fall into a state of shock or fly at one another's throats. They will jockey for position, try different devices, make many experiments. Some will find equivalent solutions. Some will give it up and busy themselves in other profitable ways. Some will persist and get through. Some will lose everything. I do not know the proportion that will collect in any of these categories. If the last one comprises many, then we shall be sad, for we will have been wrong. We should have done something. If the first category comprises many, then one or more transportation systems will have been devised and we ought not to have said that people have become umbilically attached to their cars. If the second comprises many, then we shall have discovered new urban forms. If the third comprises many, then life will hardly have changed, and we shall have found that not all aspects of congestion are pathological— indeed, some may prove capable of existing in an agreeable homeostasis. But that state of grace cannot be attained by the application of technology alone.

Aside from the complexities of the problem, if we consider only the mass of people and vehicles that must be moved, the maximum channels available, and the speed and amenities required, it becomes apparent that any uncompromising solution would violate the principle of the conservation of matter and the incompressibility of people and things. Technology has been variously invoked—wistfully, petulantly, or indignantly—to do something, as if it were possible to arrange five people and their impedimenta in the space occupied by one person. Proposals that turn in some manner on the size, organization, and ownership of vehicles and on the limitations and exclusions of travel do not pose difficult technological problems. All of them are soluble now. The debate that congestion has generated really hinges on questions of policy. I doubt whether there is any solution that will not in some sense proscribe someone's freedom to travel or that will not essentially modify the city.

Patterns of urban density and congestion are related: given the state of technology, we cannot specify either one independently of the other. Chronic congestion is a characteristic of cities, and I suspect that technology has been used to realize patterns of growth at maximum density, which is to say at maximum congestion. This policy was not a necessity but rather a choice from among other alternates, however unconsciously made. When technology was primitive, hardly any other was possible. An automobile does not fit this choice easily because at one end of its trip it becomes almost immobile, and at the other, too mobile. It shares the former disability with other vehicles during other times. The streets of ancient Rome were also too narrow to bear the traffic. But the latter disability is a new event. The city at present may exhibit the first occasion in history of a society suffering from an excess of local mobility.

The determination of modes of travel is a matter of policy, but technology can contribute much to making them easier. Nothing radical can be expected by way of new vehicles. In heavy traffic, within a range of from zero to ten miles, only a form of surface travel seems feasible. The largest advantages in this scale will probably derive from the elaboration of controls. These are the devices that will permit the most efficient use of the facilities. To design these controls would require a knowledge of traffic ranging from the micro-mechanics of congestion to the optimal properties of transportation networks in the large. The degree of control, however, would be a matter of policy. It can be as tight as the controls imposed on aircraft or as lenient as a set of street signals responding to local traffic. By themselves, controls are ambivalent with respect to patterns of density.

SUMMARY

An inadequate supply of water seems to be the only condition that may stunt the growth of cities. In all other respects, a city of fifty million is a reasonable extrapolation. The future capabilities of communication are not likely to favor any particular form of the city. Automation in production and administration will change the profile of jobs and the length of the work day. The effects may be greater on the smaller than on the larger cities. All cities will be faced with the problem of providing for the increase in leisure.

Aircraft may become the dominant mode of transportation over long distances, in which case, the relative growth of cities will depend in some measure on their position in the transportation network. If the amount of time devoted to local travel at present is to be maintained, then the span of large cities in the future makes it likely that aircraft will become a necessary component of metropolitan travel. If uncontrolled, this use of aircraft will encourage diffuse and formless growth. Local congestion, however, is not a technological problem.

The patterns of density within a city appear to be largely independent of technological developments. I think we should be unhappy if it were otherwise, for the fight for control is difficult enough as it is. Technology is now sufficiently versatile to meet most reasonable specifications. We need no longer wait and wonder.

5. The Political Implications of Metropolitan Growth

EDWARD C. BANFIELD

THE RAPID GROWTH of the metropolitan populations will not necessarily have much political effect. To be sure, many new facilities, especially schools, highways, and water supply and sewage disposal systems, will have to be built and much private activity will have to be regulated. But such things do not necessarily have anything to do with politics: the laying of a sewer pipe by a "public" body may involve the same kinds of behavior as the manufacture of the pipe by a "private" one. Difficulties that are "political" arise (and they may arise in "private" as well as in "public" undertakings) only in so far as there is conflict—conflict over what the common good requires or between what it requires and what private interests want. The general political situation is affected, therefore, not by changes in population density or in the number and complexity of the needs that government serves ("persons," the human organisms whose noses are counted by census-takers, are not necessarily "political actors") but rather by actions which increase conflict in matters of public importance or make the management of it more difficult. In what follows, such actions will be called "burdens" upon the political system.

In judging how a political system will work over time, increases and decreases in the burdens upon it are obviously extremely relevant. They are not all that must be considered, however. Changes in the "capability" of a system, that is, in its ability to manage conflict and to impose settlements, are equally relevant. The "effectiveness" of a political system is a ratio between burdens and capability. Even though the burdens upon it increase, the effectiveness of a system will also increase if there is a sufficient accompanying increase in its capability. Similarly, even though there is an increase in capability, the effectiveness of a system will decrease if there is a more than commensurate increase in burdens.

In this article an impressionistic account will be given with respect to two contrasting political systems, the British and the American, of the burdens metropolitan affairs place upon them and of their changing capabilities. Naturally, the focus of attention will be upon *ratios* of burdens to capabilities and upon the significance of these ratios for metropolitan affairs.

THE TASKS OF BRITISH LOCAL GOVERNMENT

Until recently British local government (meaning not only government that is locally controlled but all government that deals with local affairs) had, by American standards, very little to do. Until three or four years ago there was little traffic regulation in Britain because there were few cars (the first few parking meters, all set for two hours, were installed in London in the summer of 1958). Now all of a sudden there are 5,500,000 cars—more per mile of road than in any other country—and the number is increasing by a net of 1,500 per day; by 1975 there are expected to be 13,500,000. Obviously, the need for roads and parking places will be enormous. But the automobile will create other and graver problems for local government. When there are enough cars and highways, there will doubtless be a "flight to the suburbs." The central business districts will be damaged, and so will mass transit (94 per cent of those who now enter London do so by public transportation) and the green belts.[1]

Law enforcement has been relatively easy in Britain up to now. The British have not been culturally disposed toward violence or toward the kinds of vice that lead to major crimes. (There are only 450 dope addicts in all of Britain, whereas in Chicago alone there are from 12,000 to 15,000.) British opinion, moreover, has not demanded that some forms of vice be made illegal, much less that vice in general be suppressed. In England adultery is not illegal, and neither is prostitution, although it is illegal to create a nuisance by soliciting. Physicians in England may prescribe dope to addicts. (In the United States, where this is illegal, black-market prices prevail and the addict must usually resort to crime to support his habit. In Chicago a week's supply of heroin costs at least $105; to realize this much, the addict must steal goods worth about $315. According to the estimate of a criminal court judge, about $50 million worth of goods is shoplifted every year in the central business district of Chicago by addicts.[2]) Never having tried to suppress drinking, gambling, or prostitution, the British have no organized crime.

The task of law enforcement is also becoming more difficult, however. Dope addiction, and consequently crimes of violence, will increase with the number of West Indians and others who are not culturally at home in England. In the past year the horde of London prostitutes has been driven underground, where it may prove a powerful force tending toward the corruption of the police.[3] As traffic fines increase in number and amount, the bribery of the police by motorists will also increase. "All Britain's big cities," an *Observer* writer recently said, "now have enclaves of crime where the major masculine trades appear to be pimping and dealing in dubious second-hand cars."[4]

Even if motorists, dope addicts, and prostitutes do not seriously corrupt it, the police force is bound to deteriorate. The British have had extraordinarily fine policemen, partly because their social system has hitherto offered the working class few better opportunities. As it becomes easier to rise out of the working class, the police force will have to get along with less desirable types. It is significant that the Metropolitan Police are now 3,000 men short.

State-supported schooling, one of the heaviest tasks of local government in the United States, has been a comparatively easy one in Britain. Four out of five British children leave school before the age of 16. The British, it is said, are not likely to develop a taste for mass education.[5] They are demanding more and better state-supported schools, however, and no doubt the government will have to do more in this field.

It would be wrong to infer that because of these changes the burden upon the British political system will henceforth be comparable to that upon our own or, indeed, that it will increase at all. Conceivably, the new tasks of local government will have no more political significance than would, say, a doubling of the volume of mail to be carried by the post office. One can imagine, for example, two opposite treatments of the London traffic problem, one of which would solve the problem without creating any burden upon the political system and the other of which would leave the problem unsolved while creating a considerable burden.

Possibility 1. The Ministry of Transport takes jurisdiction over London traffic. Acting on the recommendations of a Royal Commission, the Minister declares that the central city will be closed to private automobiles. His decision is acclaimed as wise and fair—"the only thing to do"—by everyone who matters.

Possibility 2. The boroughs retain their control over traffic because the Minister is mindful of organized motorists. People feel that it is an outrageous infringement of the rights of Englishmen to charge for parking on the Queen's highway or to fine a motorist without having first served a summons upon him in the traditional manner. Traffic is unregulated, and everyone complains bitterly.

As this suggests, "governmental tasks" are "political burdens" only if public opinion makes them so. What would be an overwhelming burden in one society may not be any burden at all

in another. What would not be a burden upon a particular
political system at one time may become one at another. It is
essential to inquire, therefore, what changes are occurring in
the way such matters are usually viewed in Great Britain and
in the United States. The factors that are particularly relevant
in this connection include: the intensity with which ends are
held and asserted; the willingness of actors to make concessions, to subordinate private to public interests, and to accept
arbitration; and, finally, the readiness of the voters to back the
government in imposing settlements.

THE RELATION OF CITIZEN TO GOVERNMENT

The British have a very different idea than we have of the
proper relation between government and citizens. They believe
that it is the business of the government to govern. The voter
may control the government by giving or withholding consent,
but he may not participate in its affairs. The leader of the
majority in the London County Council, for example, has
ample power to carry into effect what he and his policy committee decide upon; it is taken for granted that he will make
use of his power (no one will call him a boss for doing so)
and that he will not take advice or tolerate interference from
outsiders.

Locally as well as nationally, British government has been in
the hands of the middle and upper classes. Civil servants,
drawn of course entirely from the middle class, have played
leading and sometimes dominant roles. Most elected representatives have been middle or upper class. The lower class
has not demanded, and apparently has not wanted, to be governed by its own kind or to have what in the United States is
called "recognition." Although Labour has controlled the London County Council since 1934, there have never been in the
Council any such gaudy representatives of the gutter as, for
example, Alderman "Paddy" Bauler of Chicago. The unions
have kept people with lower-class attributes, and sometimes

people of lower-class origins as well, off the ballot. They would not have done so, of course, if the lower class had had a powerful itch to have its own kind in office. (In that case the unions would themselves have been taken over by the lower class.) As Bagehot said in explaining "deferential democracy," the numerical majority "is ready, is eager to delegate its power of choosing its ruler to a certain select minority."[6]

The ordinary man's contact with government inspires him with awe and respect. (Is government respected because it pertains to the upper classes, or does causality run the other way, the upper classes being respected because of their association with government?) "The English workingman," an Englishman who read a draft of this article said, "seems to think that the assumption of governmental responsibilities calls for the solemnest of blue suits. He tends to be so overawed by his position as to be silenced by it."

The ethos of governing bodies, then, has been middle or upper class, even when most of their members have been lower class. So has that of the ordinary citizen when, literally or figuratively, he has put on his blue suit to discharge his "governmental responsibilities" at the polls.

Consequently the standards of government have been exclusively those of the middle and upper classes. There has been great concern for fair play, great respect for civil rights, and great attention to public amenities—all matters dear to middle- and upper-class hearts. At the same time there has been entire disregard for the convenience and tastes of the workingman. London pubs, for example, are required by law to close from two until six in the afternoon, not, presumably, because no one gets thirsty between those hours or because drinking then creates a special social problem, but merely because the convenience of pub keepers (who would have to remain open if competition were allowed to operate) is placed above that of their customers. Similarly, trains and buses do not leave the center of London after eleven at night, not, presumably, because no one wants to go home later, but because the people who make the rules deem it best for those who cannot afford taxis to get to bed early.

It is not simply class prejudice that accounts for these things. By common consent of the whole society the tastes of the individual count for little against prescriptive rights. When these rights pertain to the body politic—to the Crown, in the mystique—then the tastes of the individual may be disregarded entirely. Public convenience becomes everything, private convenience nothing.

As heirs of this tradition, the British town planners are in a fortunate position. They do not have to justify their schemes by consumers' preferences. It is enough for them to show that "public values" are served, for by common consent any gain in a public value, however small, outweighs any loss of consumers' satisfaction, however large. Millions of acres of land outside of London were taken to make a green belt without anyone's pointing out that workingmen are thus prevented from having small places in the country and that rents in the central city are forced up by the reduction in the supply of land. It is enough that a public amenity is being created (an amenity, incidentally, which can be enjoyed only by those having time and money to go out of London). The planning authorities of the London County Council, to cite another example of the general disregard for consumers' tastes, consider the following questions, among others, when they pass upon an application to erect a structure more than 100 feet in height:

Would it spoil the skyline of architectural groups or landscapes? Would it have a positive visual or civic significance? Would it relate satisfactorily to open spaces and the Thames? Would its illuminations at night detract from London's night scene?

It is safe to say that the planners do not weigh the value of a gain in "visual significance" against the value of a loss in "consumer satisfaction." In all probability they do not try to discover what preferences the consumer actually has in the matter. Certainly they do not make elaborate market analyses such as are customarily used in the United States in planning not only shopping places but even public buildings.

Green belts and the control of the use of land are only part of a plan of development which includes the creation of a dozen satellite towns, "decanting" the population of the metropolis, and much else. Where these sweeping plans have not been realized, it has not been because of political opposition. There has been virtually no opposition to any of these undertakings. The real estate, mercantile, banking, taxpayer, and labor union interests, which in an American city would kill such schemes before they were started, have not even made gestures of protest. The reason is not that none of them is adversely affected. It is that opposition would be futile.[7]

THE DIRECTION OF CHANGE

Obviously, a political system that can do these things can do much else besides. If the relation between government and citizen in the next half century is as it has been in the past, the "governmental tasks" that were spoken of above will not prove to be "political burdens" of much weight. One can hardly doubt, for example, which of the two ways of handling London traffic would, on this assumption, be more probable.

There is reason to think, however, that fundamental changes are occurring in the relations between government and citizen. Ordinary people in Britain are entering more into politics, and public opinion is becoming more ebullient, restive, and assertive. The lower class no longer feels exaggerated respect for its betters,[8] and if, as seems reasonable to assume, respect for public institutions and for political things has been in some way causally connected with respect for the governing classes, the ordinary man's attachment to his society may be changing in a very fundamental way. British democracy is still deferential, but it is less so than a generation ago, and before long it may be very little so.

It would not be surprising if the lower class were soon to begin wanting to have its own kind in office. Lower-class leaders would not necessarily be less mindful of the common good and of the principles of fair play than are the present middle and upper class ones, however. The ethos of the British lower class may not be as different from that of the other classes as we in America, judging others by ourselves, are likely to imagine.

There is in Britain a tendency to bring the citizen closer to the process of government. Witness, for example, a novel experiment (as the *Times* described it) tried recently by an urban district council. At the conclusion of its monthly meeting, the council invited the members of the public present (there were about twenty) to ask questions. According to the *Times:*[9]

The Council, having decided to cast themselves into the arms of the electorate, had obviously given some thought to how they could extricate themselves if the hug became an uncomfortable squeeze. The chairman, after expressing the hope that the experiment would be successful, suggested a few rules. It was undesirable, he said, that such a meeting should become an ordinary debate with members of the public debating with members of the council and perhaps members of the council debating with each other. He decreed that the public should be restricted to questions on policy or factual information. He finished the preliminaries by saying that if things got out of hand he would rise and would then expect all further discussion to cease.

This last precaution proved to be unnecessary. The public were pertinent, probing, and shrewd in their questions, but content to observe the proprieties. The more vexed of domestic questions of Nantwich (the demolition of old property, road repairs, housing, and the like) were thrown down quickly and in every case received reasoned replies. The atmosphere of the chamber continued to be one of high good humor.

Carried far enough, this kind of thing would lead to the radical weakening of government. (There is no use giving people information unless you are going to listen to their opinions. And if you do that, you are in trouble, for their opinions are not likely to be on public grounds, and they are virtually certain to conflict.) The British are not likely to develop a taste for what in American cant is called "grass-roots democracy," however; the habit of leaving things to the government and of holding the government responsible is too deeply ingrained for that. What the public wants is not the privilege of participating in the process of government but, as the Franks Committee said, "openness, fairness, and impartiality" in official proceedings.[10]

The tastes of the ordinary man (consumers' preferences) will be taken more into account in the future than they have been in the past, not because the ordinary man will demand it (he may in time, but he is far from doing so now) but because the ruling elite—an elite that will be more sophisticated in such things than formerly—will think it necessary and desirable. The efforts of the Conservative government to let the market allocate housing are a case in point. These have been motivated, not by desire to deprive the workingman of advantages he has had for half a century (that would be out of the question), but by awareness that people's tastes may be best served in a market. The cherished green belts are now being scrutinized by people who are aware of consumer demand for living space, and some planners are even beginning to wonder if there is not something to be said for the American system of zoning. It is not beyond the bounds of possibility that the British will exchange their system of controls of the use of land, which as it stands allows the planner to impose a positive conception, for something resembling ours, which permits the user of land to do as he pleases so long as he does not violate a rule of law.

The conclusion seems warranted that twenty or thirty years from now, when today's children have become political actors, governmental tasks which would not place much of a burden on the political system may then place a considerable one on it. Governmental tasks like traffic regulation will be more burdensome politically both because there will be insistent pressure to take a wider range of views and interests into ac-

count, but also, and perhaps primarily, because the ruling
group will have become convinced that the preferences of ordinary people ought to count for a great deal even when "public
values" are involved. It is not impossible that the elite may
come to attach more importance to the preferences of ordinary
people than will the ordinary people themselves.

THE CONTRASTING AMERICAN TRADITION

Local government in the United States presents a sharply
contrasting picture. It has been required to do a great deal,
and the nature of American institutions and culture has made
almost all of its tasks into political burdens.

Although there have always been among us believers in
strong central government, our governmental system, as compared to the British, has been extraordinarily weak and decentralized. This has been particularly true of state and local
government. The general idea seems to have been that no one
should govern, or failing that, that everyone should govern
together. The principle of checks and balances and the division
of power, mitigated in the federal government by the great
powers of the presidency, were carried to extreme lengths in
the cities and states. As little as fifty years ago, most cities were
governed by large councils, some of them bicameral, and by
mayors who could do little but preside over the councils. There
was no such thing as a state administration. Governors were
ceremonial figures only, and state governments were mere
congeries of independent boards and commissions. Before anything could be done, there had to occur a most elaborate
process of give and take (often, alas, in the most literal sense)
by which bits and pieces of power were gathered up temporarily, almost momentarily.

It was taken for granted that the ordinary citizen had a right
—indeed, a sacred duty—to interfere in the day-to-day conduct
of public affairs. Whereas in Britain the press and public have
been excluded from the deliberations of official bodies, in the

United States it has been common practice to require by law that all deliberations take place in meetings open to the public. Whereas in Britain the electorate is never given an opportunity to pass upon particular projects by vote, in the United States it usually is. In Los Angeles, according to James Q. Wilson, "The strategy of political conflict is more often than not based upon the assumption that the crucial decision will be made not by the City Council of Los Angeles, the Board of Supervisors of the County, or the Legislature of the state, but by the voters in a referendum election."[11]

Los Angeles is an extreme case, but the general practice of American cities, a practice required by law in many of them, is to get the voters' approval of major expenditures. The New York City government, one of the strongest, is now having to choose between building schools and making other necessary capital expenditures; it cannot do both because the voters of the state have refused to lift the constitutional limit on debt. Such a thing could not happen in London; there all such decisions are made by the authorities, *none of whom is elected at large.*

The government of American cities has for a century been almost entirely in the hands of the working class.[12] This class, moreover, has had as its conception of a desirable political system one in which people are "taken care of" with jobs, favors, and protection, and in which class and ethnic attributes get "recognition." The idea that there are values, such as efficiency, which pertain to the community as a whole and to which the private interests of individuals ought to be subordinated has never impressed the working-class voter.

The right of the citizen to have his wishes, whether for favors, "recognition," or something else, served by local government, has been an aspect of the generally privileged position of the consumer. If the British theory has been that any gain in public amenity, however small, is worth any cost in consumer satisfaction, however large, ours has been the opposite: with us, any gain to the consumer is worth any cost to the public. What the consumer is not willing to pay for is not of much value in our eyes. Probably most Americans believe that if the consumer prefers his automobile to public transportation his taste ought to be respected, even if it means the destruction of the cities.

We have, indeed, gone far beyond the ideal of admitting everyone to participation in government and of serving everyone's tastes. We have made public affairs a game which anyone may play by acting "as if" he has something at stake, and these make-believe interests become subjects of political struggle just as if they were real. "The great game of politics" has for many people a significance of the same sort as, say, the game of business or the game of social mobility. All, in fact, are parts of one big game. The local community, as Norton E. Long has maintained in a brilliant article, may be viewed as an ecology of games: the games serve certain social functions (they provide determinate goals and calculable strategies, for example, and this gives an element of coordination to what would otherwise be a chaotic pull and haul), but the real satisfaction is in "playing the game."[13]

Since the American political arena is more a playground than a forum, it is not surprising that, despite the expenditure of vast amounts of energy, problems often remain unsolved—after all, what is really wanted is not solutions but the fun of the game. Still less is it surprising that those in authority seldom try to make or impose comprehensive solutions. The mayor of an American city does not think it appropriate for him to do much more than ratify agreements reached by competing interest groups. For example, the mayor of Minneapolis does not, according to a recent report, "actively sponsor anything. He waits for private groups to agree on a project. If he likes it, he endorses it. Since he has no formal power with which to pressure the Council himself, he feels that the private groups must take the responsibility for getting their plan accepted."[14]

American cities, accordingly, seldom make and never carry out comprehensive plans. Plan making is with us an idle exercise, for we neither agree upon the content of a "public interest" that ought to override private ones nor permit the centralization of authority needed to carry a plan into effect if one were made. There is much talk of the need for metropolitan-area planning, but the talk can lead to nothing practical because there is no possibility of agreement on what the "general interest" of such an area requires concretely (whether, for example, it requires keeping the Negroes concentrated in the central city or spreading them out in the suburbs) and because, anyway, there does not exist in any area a government that could carry such plans into effect.[15]

CHANGE IN THE UNITED STATES

The relation of the citizen to the government is changing in the United States as it is in Britain. But the direction of our development is opposite to that of the British: whereas their government is becoming more responsive to popular opinion and therefore weaker, ours is becoming less responsive and therefore stronger. In state and local government this trend has been underway for more than a generation and it has carried far. Two-thirds of our smaller cities are now run by professional managers, who, in routine matters at least, act without much interference. In the large central cities, mayors have wider spheres of authority than they did a generation ago, much more and much better staff assistance (most of them have deputies for administrative management), and greater freedom from the electorate. These gains are in most cases partly offset, and in some perhaps more than partly, by the decay of party machines, which could turn graft, patronage, and other "gravy" into political power, albeit power that was seldom used to public advantage.

Reformers in America have struggled persistently to strengthen government by overcoming the fragmentation of formal authority which has afflicted it from the beginning. The council manager system, the executive budget, metropolitan

area organization—these have been intended more to increase
the ability of government to get things done (its capability, in
the terminology used above) than to make it less costly or less
corrupt.[16]

One of the devices by which power has been centralized and
the capability of government increased is the special function
district or authority. We now commonly use authorities to
build and manage turnpikes, airports and ports, redevelopment
projects, and much else. They generally come into being because the jurisdictions of existing general-purpose governments
do not coincide with the areas for which particular functions
must be administered. But if this reason for them did not exist,
they would have to be created anyway, for they provide a way
of escaping to a considerable extent the controls and interfer-
ences under which government normally labors. The authority,
as a rule, does not go before the electorate or even the legislature; it is exempt from the usual civil-service requirements,
budget controls, and auditing, and it is privileged to conduct
its affairs out of sight of the public.

The success of all these measures to strengthen government
is to be explained by the changing class character of the urban
electorate. The lower-class ideal of government, which recognized no community larger than the ward and measured advantages only in favors, "gravy," and nationality "recognition,"
has almost everywhere gone out of fashion. To be a Protestant
and a Yankee is still a political handicap in every large North-
ern city, but to be thought honest, public-spirited, and in some
degree statesmanlike is now essential. (John E. Powers, the
candidate expected by everyone to win the 1959 Boston mayor-
alty election, lost apparently because he fitted too well an
image of the Irish politician that the Irish electorate found
embarrassing and wanted to repudiate.) Many voters still
want "nationality recognition," it has been remarked, but they
want a kind that is flattering.[17] It appears to follow from this
that the nationality-minded voter prefers a candidate who has
the attributes of his group but has them in association with

those of the admired Anglo-Saxon model. The perfect candidate is of Irish, Polish, Italian, or Jewish extraction, but has the speech, dress, and manner, and also the public virtues (honesty, impartiality, devotion to the public good) that belong in the public mind to the upper-class Anglo-Saxon.

The ascendant middle-class ideal of government emphasizes "public values," especially impartiality, consistency, and efficiency. The spread of the council-manager system and of non-partisanship, the short ballot, at-large voting, and the merit system testify to the change.

Middle-class insistence upon honesty and efficiency has raised the influence and prestige of professionals in the civil service and in civic associations. These are in a position nowadays to give or withhold a good government "seal of approval" which the politician must display on his product.

The impartial expert who "gets things done" in spite of "politicians" and "pressure groups" has become a familiar figure on the urban scene and even something of a folk hero, especially among the builders, contractors, realtors, and bankers who fatten from vast construction projects.[18] Robert Moses is the outstanding example, but there are many others in smaller bailiwicks. The special function district or authority is, of course, their natural habitat; without the protection it affords from the electorate they could not survive.

The professionals, of course, favor higher levels of spending for public amenities. Their enlarged influence might in itself lead to improvements in the quality and quantity of goods and services provided publicly. But the same public opinion that has elevated the professional has also elevated the importance of these publicly-supplied goods and services. It is the upper-middle- and the lower-class voters who support public expenditure proposals (the upper-middle-class voters because they are mindful of "the good of the community" and the lower-class ones because they have everything to gain and nothing to lose by public expenditures); lower-middle-class voters, who are worried about mortgage payments, hostile toward the lower

class (which threatens to engulf them physically and otherwise), and indifferent to community-regarding values, constitute most of the opposition to public improvements of all kinds.

Thus it happens that as Britain begins to entertain doubts
about green belts, about controls of the use of land that make
much depend upon the taste of planners, and about treating
public amenity as everything and consumer satisfaction as
nothing, we are moving in the opposite direction. There is a
lively demand in the United States for green belts (the *New
York Times* recently called "self-evident truth" the astonishing
statement of an economist that "it is greatly to be doubted if
any unit of government under any circumstances has ever
bought or can ever buy too much recreation land");[19] the
courts are finding that zoning to secure aesthetic values is a
justifiable exercise of the police power; performance zoning,
which leaves a great deal to the discretion of the planner, is
becoming fashionable, and J. K. Galbraith has made it a part
of conventional wisdom to believe that much more of the national income should be spent for public amenities.

Perhaps in the next twenty or thirty years municipal affairs
will pass entirely into the hands of honest, impartial, and non-
political "experts"; at any rate, this seems to be the logical ful-
fillment of the middle-class ideal. If the ideal is achieved, the
voters will accept, from a sense of duty to the common good,
whatever the experts say is required. We may see in the present
willingness of business and civic leaders to take at face value
the proposals being made by professionals for master planning, metropolitan organization, and the like, and in the
exalted position of Robert Moses of New York, portents of what
is to come.

The presence in the central cities of large numbers of
Negroes, Puerto Ricans, and white hillbillies creates a cross-
current of some importance. For a generation, at least, these
newcomers will prefer the old-style politics of the ward boss
and his "gravy train." How this anomaly will fit into the larger
pattern of middle-class politics is hard to imagine. Possibly

the lower class will simply be denied representation. And possibly the rate of increase of per capita income being what it is, the assimilation of these people into the middle class will take place faster than anyone now imagines.

SUMMARY AND CONCLUSIONS

It has been argued in this paper that the tasks a government must perform (the number and complexity of goods and services it must supply) have no necessary relation to political matters. Tasks may increase without accompanying increases in the burden placed upon a political system. The important questions for political analysis, therefore, concern not population density or other indicators of the demand for goods and services, but rather the amount and intensity of conflict and the capacity of the government for managing it. Looked at from this standpoint, it appears that the effectiveness of British government in matters of local concern will probably decrease somewhat over the long run. The demands that will be made upon it in the next generation will be vastly more burdensome than those of the recent past (although also vastly less burdensome than the same demands would be in America), and the capacity of the government will be somewhat less. The effectiveness of local government in the United States, on the other hand, will probably increase somewhat. Local government has had more tasks to perform here than in Britain, and these have imposed enormously greater burdens. The tasks of local government will doubtless increase here too in the next generation, but the burdens they impose will probably decline. American local government is becoming stronger and readier to assert the paramountcy of the public interest, real or alleged.

Although each system has moved a considerable distance in the direction of the other, they remain far apart and each retains its original character. The British, although more sensitive to public opinion, still believe that the government should govern. And we, although acknowledging that the development of metropolitan areas should be planned, still believe that everyone has a right to "get in on the act" and to make his influence felt. Obviously, the differences are crucial, and although the trend seems to be toward greater effectiveness here and toward reduced effectiveness in Britain, there can be no doubt that in absolute terms the effectiveness of the British system is and will remain far greater than that of ours. Despite the increase in the tasks it must perform, the burden upon it will remain low by American standards, and its capability will remain high. Matters which would cause great political difficulty here will probably be easily settled there.

The basic dynamic principle in both systems has not been change in population density but rather change in class structure and outlook. It is the relaxation of the bonds of status that has caused the British workingman to enter more into politics, that has made his tastes and views count for more, and that has raised questions about the right of an elite to decide matters. In America the assimilation of the lower class to the middle class and the consequent spread of an ideal of government which stresses honesty, impartiality, efficiency, and regard for public as well as private interest have encouraged the general strengthening of government.

The mere absence of dispute, acrimony, unworkable compromise, and stalemate (this, after all, is essentially what the concept "effectiveness" refers to in this connection) ought not, of course, to be taken as constituting a "good" political order. Arrogant officials may ignore the needs and wishes of ordinary citizens, and the ordinary citizens may respectfully acquiesce in their doing so, either because they think (as the British lower class does) that the gentleman knows best or (as the American middle class does) that the expert knows best. In such cases there may be great effectiveness—no dispute, no acrimony, no unworkable compromise, no stalemate—but far from signifying that the general welfare is being served, such a state of affairs signifies instead that the needs and wishes with which welfare under ordinary circumstances, especially in local matters, is largely concerned are not being taken into account. To say, then, that our system is becoming somewhat more and the British system somewhat less effective does not by any means imply "improvement" for us and the opposite for them. It is quite conceivable that dispute, acrimony, unworkable compromise, and stalemate may be conspicuous features of any situation that approximates the ideal of general welfare.

Such conclusions, resting as they do on rough and, at best, common-sense assessments, amply illustrate the difficulty of prediction, and—since the causal principles lie deep in social structure and in culture—the utter impossibility within a free society of a foresighted control of such matters.

REFERENCES

1. Dame Evelyn Sharp, Permanent Secretary, Ministry of Housing and Local Government, recently pointed out that the expected population increase in England and Wales in the next 15 years (nearly three million) is almost double the increase on which plans have been based. The number of separate households, moreover, is growing faster than the number of people. Much of the demand for new housing, she said, is demand for better and more spacious housing. All this has increased the pressure on land, especially on the green belt, and particularly around London. The Government policy, she said, was to encourage the building of houses for owner occupation, and how to follow this without wrecking the effort to preserve the green belt was one of the most difficult problems facing the planning authorities. She said there were also increasing demands on land by industry, for great new roads, car parking and garaging, and for power. The *Times*, October 23, 1959.

2. These facts were supplied by Dr. Arnold Abrams of Chicago in a private communication.

3. The Wolfenden Committee considered this possibility and concluded that the measures it proposed (chiefly to make it easier for police officers to establish "annoyance") justified the risk. Its measures, the Committee said, were not "likely to result in markedly increased corruption. There are other fields of crime where the temptation to the police to succumb to bribery is, and will continue to be, much stronger than it is here." *Report of the Committee on Homosexual Offenses and Prostitution,* Cmnd. 247, September 1957, p. 96.

4. "Table Talk," *The Observer,* May 15, 1960.

5. Sir Geoffrey Crowther, "English and American Education," *The Atlantic,* April 1960.

6. Walter Bagehot, *The English Constitution* (New York: Oxford University Press, 1928), ch. 9.

7. An English friend comments: "I think you underestimate the sensitivity of central government to local or even private pressures. Parliamentary questions and debates, M.P.s' correspondence, lobbying, etc., provide plenty of opportunity for needling Ministers. The difference [between American and British practice] is, I think, that in Britain the government is not necessarily deflected by the pressures although it does its best to placate them. It does *not* ride rough-shod over protests; it lumbers on,

writhing under the criticism and dispensing half-baked compromises."

8. Such an incident as the following, which is supposed to have occurred about the time of the First World War, would be inconceivable today: Hulme [the poet] was making water in Soho Square in broad daylight when a policeman came up. "You can't do that here." Hulme: "Do you realize you're addressing a member of the middle class?" at which the policeman murmured, "Beg pardon, sir," and went on his beat. Christopher Hassall, *Edward Marsh, Patron of the Arts: A Biography* (London: Longmans, Green, 1959), p. 187.

9. The *Times,* November 24, 1959.

10. *Report of the Committee on Administrative Tribunals and Enquiries,* Cmnd. 218, July 1958.

11. James Q. Wilson, *A Report on Politics in Los Angeles,* Joint Center for Urban Studies of Massachusetts Institute of Technology and Harvard University, 1959, pp. 1-13.

12. A couple of generations ago politics was literally the principal form of mass entertainment. See Mayor Curley's account of the Piano-Smashing Contest, Peg-Leg Russell, the greased-pig snatch, and other such goings-on at Caledonian Grove. When the working class could pay more than twenty-five cents for its all-day family outing, it went to Fenway Park and baseball pushed politics into second place. James M. Curley, *I'd Do It Again!* (New York: Prentice-Hall, 1957), pp. 54-55.

13. Norton E. Long, "The Local Community as an Ecology of Games," *American Journal of Sociology,* 1958, 64: 252.

14. Alan Altshuler, *A Report on Politics in Minneapolis* (Cambridge, Joint Center for Urban Studies of Massachusetts Institute of Technology and Harvard University, 1959), pp. 11-14. The writer has described the posture of Mayor Daley of Chicago, the undisputed boss of a powerful machine, in similar terms. This suggests that it is not lack of power so much as a sense of what is seemly that prevents American mayors from taking a strong line. See E. C. Banfield, *Political Influence* (Chicago: The Free Press, forthcoming), ch. 9.

15. See E. C. Banfield and M. Grodzins, *Government and Housing in Metropolitan Areas* (New York: McGraw-Hill, 1958), esp. chs. 3 and 4.

16. See Don K. Price, "The Promotion of the City Manager Plan," *Public Opinion Quarterly,* Winter 1941, pp. 563-578.

17. In a study of politics in Worcester, Massachusetts, Robert H. Binstock has written: "Israel Katz, like Casdin, is a Jewish

Democrat now serving his fourth term on the Worcester City Council. Although he is much more identifiably Jewish than Casdin, he gets little ethnic support at the polls; there is a lack of rapport between him and the Jewish voter. The voter apparently wants to transcend many features of his ethnic identification and therefore rejects candidates who fit the stereotype of the Jew too well. Casdin is an assimilated Jew in Ivy-League clothes; Katz, by contrast, is old-world rather than new, clannish rather than civic-minded, and penny-pinching rather than liberal. Non-Jews call Katz a 'character,' Casdin a 'leader.' It is not too much to say that the Jews, like other minorities, want a flattering, not an unflattering, mirror held up to them." (Robert H. Binstock, *A Report on the Politics of Worcester,* Joint Center for Urban Studies of Massachusetts Institute of Technology and Harvard University, forthcoming, 1960, Section II, B, 2.)

18. "In our political or business or labor organizations," Robert E. Sherwood observes in his account of Roosevelt and Hopkins, "we are comforted by the knowledge that at the top is a Big Boss whom we are free to revere or to hate and upon whom we can depend for quick decisions when the going gets tough. The same is true of our Boy Scout troops and our criminal gangs. It is most conspicuously true of our passion for competitive sport. We are trained from childhood to look to the coach for authority in emergencies. The masterminding coach who can send in substitutes with instructions whenever he feels like it— or even send in an entirely new team—is a purely American phenomenon. In British football the team must play through the game with the same eleven men with which it started and with no orders from the sidelines; if a man is injured and forced to leave the field the team goes on playing with only ten men. In British sport, there are no Knute Rocknes or Connie Macks, whereas in American sport the mastermind is considered as an essential in the relentless pursuit of superiority." Robert E. Sherwood, *Roosevelt and Hopkins, An Intimate History* (New York: Harper & Brothers, 1948), p. 39.

19. *New York Times,* editorial, April 11, 1960. The economist was Dr. Marion Clawson of Resources for the Future, whose statement appeared in a report sponsored by the New York Metropolitan Regional Council and the New York Regional Plan Association.

6. The Pattern of the Metropolis

KEVIN LYNCH

THE PATTERN OF urban development critically affects a surprising number of problems, by reason of the spacing of buildings, the location of activities, the disposition of the lines of circulation. Some of these problems might be eliminated if only we would begin to coordinate metropolitan development so as to balance services and growth, prevent premature abandonment or inefficient use, and see that decisions do not negate one another. In such cases, the form of the urban area, whether concentrated or dispersed, becomes of relatively minor importance.

There are other problems, however, that are subtler and go deeper. Their degree of seriousness seems to be related to the particular pattern of development which has arisen. To understand these problems we must begin by evaluating the possible alternatives of metropolitan form. Therefore, consider the form of the metropolis as if it existed in a world free of pressures or special interests and on the assumption that massive forces can be harnessed for reshaping the metropolis for the common good—provided this good can be discovered. How should such power be applied?

We begin by deciding which aspects of the metropolitan pattern are crucial. We can then review the commonly recognized alternative patterns, as well as the criteria that might persuade us to choose one over another. Finally, we may hope to see the question as a whole. Then we will be ready to suggest new alternatives, and we will have a technique for choosing the best one for any particular purpose.

THE CRITICAL ASPECTS OF METROPOLITAN FORM

There are at least three vital factors in assessing the adequacy of the form of the metropolis, once its total size is known. The first of all is the magnitude and pattern of both the structural density (the ratio of floor space in buildings to the area of the site) and the structural condition (the state of obsolescence or repair). These aspects can be illustrated on a map by plotting the locations of the various classes of density ranging from high concentration to wide dispersion, and the various classes of structural condition ranging from poor to excellent. Density and condition provide a fundamental index of the physical resources an urban region possesses.

A second factor is the capacity, type, and pattern of the facilities for the circulation of persons: roads, railways, airlines, transit systems, and pathways of all sorts. Circulation and intercommunication perhaps constitute the most essential function of a city, and the free movement of persons happens to be the most difficult kind of circulation to achieve, the service most susceptible to malfunction in large urban areas.

The third factor that makes up the spatial pattern of a city is the location of fixed activities that draw on or serve large portions of the population, such as large department stores, factories, office and government buildings, warehouses, colleges, hospitals, theatres, parks, and museums. The spatial pattern of a city is made up of the location of fixed activities as well as the patterns of circulation and physical structure. However, the distribution of locally based activities, such as residence, local shopping, neighborhood services, elementary and high schools, is for our purpose sufficiently indicated by mapping the density of people or of buildings. Hence, if we have already specified structural density and the circulation system, the remaining critical fact at the metropolitan scale is the location of the city-wide activities which interact with large portions of the whole.

When we come to analyze any one of these three elements of spatial pattern, we find that the most significant features of such patterns are the grain (the degree of intimacy with which different elements, such as stores and houses, are intermixed), the focal organization (the interrelation of the nodes of concentration and interchange as contrasted with the general background), and the accessibility (the general proximity in terms of time of all points in the region to a given kind of activity or facility). In this sense, one might judge that from every point the accessibility to drugstores was low, uneven, or uniformly high, or that it varied in some regular way, for example, high at the center and low at the periphery of the region. All three aspects of pattern (focal organization, grain, and accessibility) can be mapped, and the latter two can be treated quantitatively if desired.

It is often said that the metropolis today is deficient as a living environment. It has suffered from uncontrolled development, from too rapid growth and change, from obsolescence and instability. Circulation is congested, requiring substantial time and a major effort. Accessibility is uneven, particularly to open rural land. The use of facilities is unbalanced, and they become increasingly obsolete. Residential segregation according to social groups seems to be growing, while the choice of residence for the individual remains restricted and unsatisfactory. The pattern of activities is unstable, and running costs are high. Visually, the city is characterless and confused, as well as noisy and uncomfortable.

Yet the metropolis has tremendous economic and social advantages that override its problems and induce millions to bear with the discomforts. Rather than dwindle or collapse, it is more likely to become the normal human habitat. If so, the question then is, what particular patterns can best realize the potential of metropolitan life?

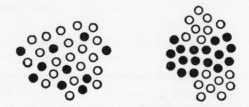

Fig. 1. Grain.

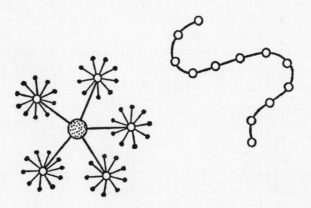

Fig. 2. Focal Organization.

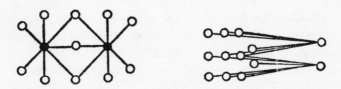

Fig. 3. Accessibility.

THE DISPERSED SHEET

One alternative is to allow the present growth at the periphery to proceed to its logical conclusion but at a more rapid pace. Let new growth occur at the lowest densities practicable, with substantial interstices of open land kept in reserve. Let older sections be rebuilt at much lower densities, so that the metropolitan region would rapidly spread over a vast continuous tract, perhaps coextensive with adjacent metropolitan

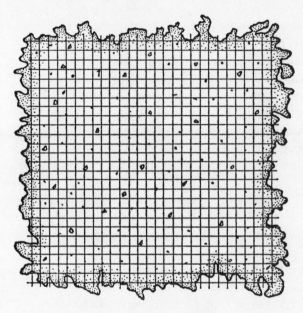

Fig. 4. The Dispersed Sheet.

regions. At the low densities of the outer suburbs, a metropolis of twenty million might require a circle of land one hundred miles in diameter.

The old center and most subcenters could be dissolved, allowing city-wide activities to disperse throughout the region, with a fine grain. Factories, offices, museums, universities, hospitals would appear everywhere in the suburban landscape. The low density and the dispersion of activities would depend on and allow circulation in individual vehicles, as well as a substantial use of distant symbolic communication such as telephone, television, mail, coded messages. Accessibility to

rural land would become unnecessary, since outdoor recreational facilities would be plentiful and close at hand. The
permanent low-density residence would displace the summer
cottage.

The system of flow, concerned solely with individual land
(and perhaps air) vehicles, should be highly dispersed in a
continuous grid designed for an even movement in all directions. There would be no outstanding nodal points, no major
terminals. Since different densities or activities would therefore
be associated in a very fine grain, the physical pattern similarly
might encourage a balanced cross-section of the population at
any given point. Work place and residence might be adjacent
or miles apart. Automatic factories and intensive food production might be dispersed throughout the region.

Frank Lloyd Wright dreamed of such a world in his Broadacre City.[1] It is this pattern toward which cities like Los
Angeles appear to be moving, although they are hampered
and corrupted by the vestiges of older city forms. Such a pattern might not only raise flexibility, local participation, personal
comfort, and independence to a maximum, but also go far
toward solving traffic congestion through the total dispersion
and balancing of loads. Its cost would be high, however, and
distances remain long. Accessibility would be good, given high
speeds of travel and low terminal times (convenient parking,
rapid starting); at the very least it would be evenly distributed.
Thus communication in the sense of purposeful trips ("I am
going out to buy a fur coat") might not be hindered, but
spontaneous or accidental communication ("Oh, look at that
fur coat in the window!"), which is one of the advantages of
present city life, might be impaired by the lack of concentration.

Although such a pattern would require massive movements
of the population and the extensive abandonment of equipment at the beginning, in the end it might promote population
stability and the conservation of resources, since all areas
would be favored alike. It gives no promise, however, of

heightening the sense of political identity in the metropolitan community nor of producing a visually vivid and well-knit image of environment. Moreover, the choice of the type of

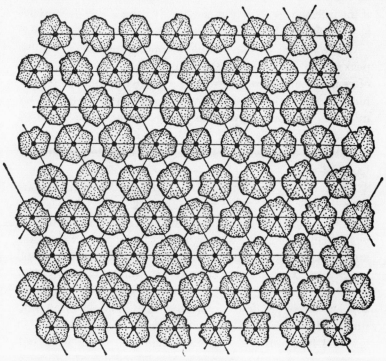

Fig. 5. The Galaxy.

residence would be restricted, although the choice of facility to be patronized (churches, stores, etc.) might be sufficiently wide.

THE GALAXY OF SETTLEMENTS

We might follow a slightly different tack while at the same time encouraging dispersion. Instead of guiding growth into an even distribution, let development be bunched into relatively small units, each with an internal peak of density and each separated from the next by a zone of low or zero structural density. Depending on the transport system, this separation might be as great as several miles. The ground occupied by the whole metropolis would increase proportionately; even if the interspaces were of minimum size, the linear dimensions of the metropolis would increase from thirty to fifty per cent.

City-wide activities could also be concentrated at the density peak within each urban cluster, thus forming an over-all system of centers, each of which would be relatively equal in importance to any of the others. Such a metropolitan pattern may be called an "urban galaxy." The centers might be balanced in composition or they might vary by specializing in a type of activity, so that one might be a cultural center, another a financial center.

The system of flow would also be dispersed but would converge locally at the center of each cluster. It might be organized in a triangular grid, which provides such a series of foci while maintaining an easy flow in all directions over the total area. Since median densities remain low, while the centers of activity are divided into relatively small units, the individual vehicle must be the major mode of transportation, but some supplementary public transportation such as buses or aircraft running from center to center would now be feasible.

While it retains many of the advantages of the dispersed sheet, such as comfort, independence, and stability, this scheme probably enhances general communication, and certainly spontaneous communication, through creating centers of activity. It would presumably encourage participation in local affairs by favoring the organization of small communities, though this might equally work against participation and coordination on the metropolitan scale. In the same sense, the visual image at the local level would be sharpened, though the metropolitan image might be only slightly improved. Flexibility might be lost, since local clusters would of necessity have relatively fixed boundaries, if interstitial spaces were preserved, and the city-wide activities would be confined to one kind of location.

The factor of time-distance might remain rather high, unless people could be persuaded to work and shop within their own cluster, which would then become relatively independent with regard to commutation. Such independent communities, of course, would largely negate many metropolitan advantages: choice of work for the employee, choice of social contacts, of services, and so on. If the transportation system were very good, then "independence" would be difficult to enforce.

This pattern, however, can be considered without assuming such local independence. It is essentially the proposal advocated by the proponents of satellite towns, pushed to a more radical conclusion, as in Clarence Stein's diagram.[2] Some of its features would appear to have been incorporated into the contemporary development of Stockholm.

The pattern of an urban galaxy provides a wider range of choice than does pure dispersion, and a greater accessibility to open country, of the kind that can be maintained between clusters. This pattern has a somewhat parochial complexion and lacks the opportunities for intensive, spontaneous communication and for the very specialized activities that might exist in larger centers. Local centers, too, might develop a monotonous similarity, unless they were given some specific individuality. That might not be easy, however, since central activities tend to support and depend on one another (wholesaling and entertainment, government and business services, headquarters offices and shopping). A compromise would be the satellite proposal proper: a swarm of such unit clusters around an older metropolitan mass.

THE CORE CITY

Those who are enamored with the advantages of concentration favor a completely opposite policy, one that would set median structural densities fairly high, perhaps at 1.0 instead of 0.1. (In other words, let there be as much interior floor space in buildings as there is total ground area in the city, instead of only one-tenth as much.) If we consider the open land that must be set aside for streets, parks, and other such uses, this means in practice the construction of elevator apartments instead of one-family houses. The metropolis would then be packed into one continuous body, with a very intensive peak of density and activity at its center. A metropolis of twenty million could be put within a circle ten miles in radius, under the building practice normal today.

FIG. 6. The Core.

Parts of the city might even become "solid," with a continuous occupation of space in three dimensions and a cubical grid of transportation lines. (The full application of this plan could cram a metropolis within a surprisingly small compass: twenty million people, with generous spacing, could be accommodated within a cube less than three miles on a side.) Most probably there would be a fine grain of specialized activities, all at high intensity, so that apartments would occur over factories, or there might also be stores on upper levels. The system of flow would necessarily be highly specialized, sorting each kind of traffic into its own channel. Such a city would depend almost entirely on public transport, rather than individual vehicles, or on devices that facilitated pedestrian movement, such as moving sidewalks or flying belts. Accessibility would be very high, both to special activities and to the open country at the edges of the city. Each family might have a second house for weekends; these would be widely dispersed throughout the countryside and used regularly three or four days during the week, or even longer, by mothers and their young children. The city itself, then, would evolve into a place for periodic gathering. Some of the great European cities, such as Paris or Moscow, which are currently building large numbers of high-density housing as compact extensions to their peripheries, are approximating this pattern without its more radical features.

Such a pattern would have an effect on living quite different from that of the previous solutions. Spontaneous communication would be high, so high that it might become necessary to impede it so as to preserve privacy. Accessibility would be excellent and time-distance low, although the channels might be crowded. The high density might increase discomfort because of noise or poor climate, although these problems could perhaps be met by the invention of new technical devices. As with the previous patterns, the choice of habitat would be restricted to a single general type within the city proper, although the population could enjoy a strong contrast on weekends or holidays. The nearness of open country and the many kinds of special services should on the whole extend individual choice. Once established, the pattern should be stable, since each point would be a highly favored location. However, a very great dislocation of people and equipment, in this country at least, would be required to achieve this pattern.

Such a metropolis would indeed produce a vivid image and would contribute to a strong sense of the community as a whole. Individual participation, on the other hand, might be very difficult. It is not clear how running costs would be affected; perhaps they would be lower because of the more efficient use of services and transportation, but initial costs would undoubtedly be very high. The segregation of social groups, as far as physical disposition can influence it, might be discouraged, although there is a level of density above which intercommunication among people begins to decline again. Certainly this solution is a highly rigid and unadaptable one in which change of function could be brought about only by a costly rearrangement.

THE URBAN STAR

A fourth proposal would retain the dominant core without so drastic a reversion to the compact city. Present densities would be kept, or perhaps revised upward a little, while low-density development at the outer fringe would no longer be allowed. Tongues of open land would be incorporated into

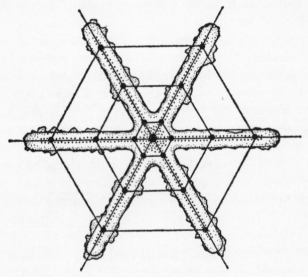

FIG. 7. The Star.

the metropolitan area to produce a density pattern that is star-shaped in the central region and linear at the fringes. These lines of dense development along the radials might in time extend to other metropolitan centers, thus becoming linear cities between the main centers. The dominant core, however, would remain, surrounded by a series of secondary centers distributed along the main radials. At moderate densities(less than the core pattern, and more than the sheet), the radial arms of a metropolis of comparable size might extend for fifty miles from its own center.

The metropolitan center of the star pattern would again contain the most intensive types of city-wide activity. Elsewhere, either in the subcenters or in linear formations along the main radials—whichever proved the more suitable—these activities would be carried on at a less intense level. The system of flow would logically be organized on the same radial pattern, with supplementary concentric rings. An efficient public transportation system of high capacity could operate along the main radials, whereas the ring roads could accommodate public transit of lower intensity. To some degree, travel by individual vehicles, although discouraged for centrally bound flows, would be practicable in other directions.

This pattern is a rationalization of the manner in which metropolitan areas were developing till the individual vehicle became the usual means of travel. It is the form the city of Copenhagen has adopted as its pattern for future growth;[3] Blumenfeld has discussed it at length.[4] This form retains the central core with its advantages of rapid communication and specialized services yet permits the location of other kinds of major activities. Lower residential densities are also possible. Individual choice should be fairly wide, both in regard to living habitat, access to services, and access to open land— this land lies directly behind each tongue of development, even at the core, and leads continuously outward to true rural land.

Movement along a sector would be fairly fast and efficient, although terminals at the core might continue to be congested and, with continued growth, the main radials might become overloaded. Movement between sectors, however, would be less favored, especially in the outer regions; there distances are great, transit hard to maintain, and channels costly, since they would span long distances over land they do not directly serve. Accessibility to services would be unequal as between inner and outer locations.

The visual image is potentially a strong one and should be conducive to a sense of the metropolis as a whole, or at least to the sense of one unified sector leading up to a common center. Growth could occur radially outward, and future change could be accomplished with less difficulty than in the compact pattern, since densities would be lower and open land would back up each strip of development. The principal problems with this form are probably those of circumferential movement, of potential congestion at the core and along the main radials, and of the wide dispersion of the pattern as it recedes from the original center.

THE RING

In the foregoing, the most discussed alternatives for metropolitan growth have been given in a highly simplified form. Other possibilities certainly exist—e.g., the compact high-density core pattern might be turned inside out, producing a doughnut-like form. In this case the center would be kept open, or at very low density, while high densities and special activities surround it, like the rim of a wheel. The principal channels of the flow system would then be a series of annular rings serving the high-intensity rim, supplemented by a set of feeder radials that would converge at the empty center. In fact, this is essentially a linear system, but one that circles back on itself and is bypassed by the "spokes" crossing the "hub." This system is well-adapted to public transportation, both on the ring roads and the cross radials, while individual vehicles might be used for circulation outside the rim.

Densities along the rim would have to be rather high, while those beyond the rim could be low. A system of weekend houses might also be effectively employed here. The central area could either be kept quite open or devoted to special uses at low densities. City-wide activities could be spotted round the rim in a series of intense centers, supplemented by linear patterns along the annular roadways. There would be no single dominant center but rather a limited number of strong centers (an aristocracy rather than a monarchy). These centers might also be specialized in regard to activity—finance, government, culture, etc.

This pseudo-linear form, like the radial tongues of the star plan, has the linear advantages: a high accessibility, both to services and to open land; a wide choice of habitat and loca-

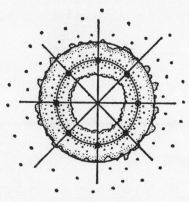

FIG. 8. The Ring.

tion of activities; and a good foundation for efficient public transit. Congestion at any single center is avoided, yet there is a high concentration. In contrast to the galaxy or satellite form, the variety and strong character inherent in the specialized centers would have some hope of survival because of the relatively close proximity of these centers.

The visual image would be strong (though perhaps a little confusing because of its circularity), producing a clear impression of the centers around the rim in contrast to the central openness, and of the way they connected with each other in sequence. The whole metropolis would seem more nearly like one community. One of the most difficult problems would be that of growth, since much development beyond the rim would soon blur the contour and require a new transportation system. A second concentric ring might be developed beyond the first, but it would negate some of the advantages of the first ring and would demand massive initiative by the central govern-

ment to undertake its development. Another difficulty would
be that of control. How can the belts of open land or the accessible center be kept free of building? Even if this problem
were solved satisfactorily, a dilemma is also likely to arise in
regard to the size of the ring: should it be small enough for
the major centers to be in close proximity to one another or big
enough to allow all the residences and other local activities to
be related to it?

One classic example of this form exists, although on a very
large scale—the ring of specialized Dutch cities that surround
a central area of agricultural land: Haarlem, Amsterdam,
Utrecht, Rotterdam, The Hague, and Leiden. This general
pattern is now being rationalized and preserved as a matter of
national policy in the Netherlands. In our own country, the
San Francisco Bay region appears to be developing in this
same direction.

The ring tends to be rather rigid and unadaptable as a form.
It would require an extreme reshaping of the present metropolis, particularly with regard to transportation and the
central business district; but it might dovetail with an observable trend toward emptying and abandoning the central areas.
The plan could be modified by retaining a single major center,
separated by a wide belt of open space from all other city-wide
activities to be disposed along the rim. It may be noted that
this use of open land in concentric belts ("green belts") is
exactly opposite to its use as radial tongues in the star form.

THE OBJECTIVES OF
METROPOLITAN ARRANGEMENT

Many other metropolitan forms are hypothetically possible,
but the five patterns described (the sheet, the galaxy, the core,
the star, and the ring) indicate the variation possible. One of
the interesting results of the discussion is to see the appearance
of a particular set of values as criteria for evaluating these
forms. It begins to be clear that some human objectives are

intimately connected with the physical pattern of a city, while others are very little affected by it. For example, there has been little discussion of the healthfulness of the environment or of its safety. Although these factors are influenced by the detailed design of the environment, such as the spacing of buildings or the provision for utilities, it is not obvious that the specific metropolitan pattern has any significant effect on them so long as we keep well ahead of the problems of pollution and supply. Psychological well-being, on the other hand, may be affected by the shape of the urban environment. But again, we are too ignorant of this aspect at present to discuss it further.

We have not referred to the efficiency of the environment in regard to production and distribution. This represents another basic criterion that probably is substantially affected by metropolitan pattern, but unfortunately no one seems to know what the effect is. "Pleasure" and "beauty" have not been mentioned, but these terms are nebulous and hard to apply accurately. A number of criteria have appeared, however, and it may well be worth while to summarize them. They might be considered the goals of metropolitan form, its fundamental objectives, either facilitated or frustrated in some significant way by the physical pattern of the metropolis.

The criterion of choice heads the list. As far as possible, the individual should have the greatest variety of goods, services, and facilities readily accessible to him. He should be able to choose the kind of habitat he prefers; he should be able to enter many kinds of environment at will, including the open country; he should have the maximum of personal control over his world. These advantages appear in an environment of great variety and of fine grain, one in which transportation and communication are as quick and effortless as possible. There may very likely be some eventual limit to the desirable increase of choice, since people can be overloaded by too many alternatives, but we do not as yet operate near that limit for most people. In practice, of course, to maximize one choice may entail minimizing another, and compromises will have to be made.

The ideal of personal interaction ranks as high as choice, although it is not quite so clear how the optimum should be defined. We often say that we want the greatest number of social contacts, so as to promote neighborliness and community organization, minimize segregation and social isolation, increase the velocity and decrease the effort of social exchange. And yet, while the evils of isolation are known, we are nevertheless beginning to see problems at the other end of the scale as well. Too much personal communication may cause breakdown, just as surely as too little. Even in moderate quantities, constant "neighborliness" can interfere with other valuable activities such as reflection, independent thought, or creative work. A high level of local community organization may mean civic indifference or intergovernmental rivalry when the large community is involved.

In this dilemma, a compromise could be found in saying that potential interaction between people should be as high as possible, as long as the individual can control it and shield himself whenever desired. His front door, figuratively speaking, should open on a bustling square, and his back door on a secluded park. Thus this ideal is seen as related to the ideal of choice.

Put differently, individuals require a rhythmical alternation of stimulus and rest—periods when personal interchange is high and to some degree is forced upon them, to be followed by other periods when stimulus is low and individually controlled. A potentially high level of interaction, individually controlled, is not the whole story; we also need some degree of spontaneous or unpremeditated exchange, of the kind that is so often useful in making new associations.

The goal of interaction, therefore, is forwarded by many of the same physical features as the goal of choice: variety, fine grain, efficient communication; but it puts special emphasis on the oscillation between stimulus and repose (centers of high activity versus quiet parks), and requires that communication be controllable. In addition, it calls for situations conducive to spontaneous exchange. Storehouses of communication, such as libraries or museums, should be highly accessible and inviting, their exterior forms clearly articulated and expressive of their function.

These two objectives of choice and interaction may be the most important goals of metropolitan form, but there are others of major importance, such as minimum first cost and minimum operating cost. These seem to depend particularly on continuous occupation along the major transportation channels, on a balanced use of the flow system, both in regard to time and direction of flow, a moderately high structural density, and a maximum reliance on collective transport.

Objectives of comfort, on the other hand, related principally to a good climate, the absence of distracting noise, and adequate indoor and outdoor space, may point either toward generally lower densities or toward expensive ameliorative works, such as sound barriers, air conditioning, and roof-top play areas. The important goal of individual participation may also indicate lower densities and an environment that promotes an active relation between an individual and his social and physical milieu, thus giving him a world that to some extent he can manage and modify by his own initiative.

We must also consider that the urban pattern will necessarily shift and expand, and therefore it is important to ask whether the adjustment to new functions will be relatively easy, and whether growth, as well as the initial state, is achievable with a minimum of control and central initiative and intervention. Adaptability to change seems to be greater at lower densities, since scattered small structures are readily demolished or converted. Both an efficient transport system and some form of separation of one kind of activity from another are also conducive to flexibility. Discontinuous forms like the galaxy or the ring require special efforts to control growth, for these patterns raise problems such as the appearance of squatters and the preservation and use of intervening open land.

Stability is a somewhat contradictory goal; it takes into account the critical social and economic costs of obsolescence, movement of population, and change of function. It is very possible that stability in the modern world will be impossible to maintain, and it runs counter to many of the values cited above. The criterion of stability may then be restated: if change is inevitable, it should be moderated and controlled so as to prevent violent dislocations and preserve a maximum of continuity with the past. This criterion would have important implications as to how the metropolis should grow and change.

Finally, there are many esthetic goals the metropolis can satisfy. The most clear-cut is that the metropolis should be "imageable," that is, it should be visually vivid and well structured; its component parts should be easily recognized and easily interrelated. This objective would encourage the use of intensive centers, variety, sharp grain (clear outlines between parts), and a differentiated but well-patterned flow system.

THE RELATION OF FORMS TO GOALS

We have now treated a number of objectives that are crucial, that are on the whole rather generally accepted, and that seem to be significantly affected by the pattern of the metropolis: the goals of choice, interaction, cost, comfort, participation, growth and adaptability, continuity, and imageability. Other goals may develop as we increase our knowledge of city form. What even these few imply for city form is not yet obvious; moreover, they often conflict, as when interaction and cost appear to call for higher densities, while comfort, participation, and adaptability achieve optimal realization at lower levels. Nevertheless, we have immediate decisions to make regarding the growth of urban areas, and if we marshall our goals and our alternatives as best we can, we can the better make these decisions.

The clarifying of alternatives and objectives has an obvious value, for this will permit public debate and the speculative analysis of the probable results of policy as related to any given form. Yet this kind of approach will soon reach a limit of usefulness unless it is supported by experimental data. Such experimentation is peculiarly difficult in regard to so large and complex an organism as a metropolis. To some degree we can form judgments drawn from such different urban regions as Los Angeles, Stockholm, and Paris, but these judgments are necessarily distorted by various cultural and environmental disparities. Possibly we can study certain partial aspects of city form, such as the effects of varying density or the varying composition of centers, but the key questions pertain to the metropolitan pattern as an operating whole. Since we cannot build a metropolis purely for experimental purposes, we can only build and test models, with some simplified code to designate pattern. By simulating basic urban functions in these models, tests might be run for such criteria as cost, accessibility, imageability, or adaptability. Such tests will be hard to relate to the real situation, and it is difficult to see how certain objectives (such as interaction or participation) can be tested, yet this technique is our best current hope for experimental data on the implications of the total metropolitan pattern.

DYNAMIC AND COMPLEX FORMS

Until we have such experimental data, what can we conclude from our imaginary juxtaposition of metropolitan form and human goals? Each of the alternatives proposed has its drawbacks, its failures in meeting some basic objectives. A radical, consistent dispersion of the metropolis appears to restrict choice, impair spontaneous interaction, entail high cost, and inhibit a vivid metropolitan image. A galaxy of small communities promises better, but would still be substandard as regards choice, interaction, and cost, besides being harder to realize. A recentralization of the metropolis in an intensive core appears to entail almost fatal disadvantages in cost, comfort, individual participation, and adaptability. The rationalization of the old metropolis in a star would work better if central congestion could be avoided and free accessibility maintained, but this form is less and less usable as size increases. The ring has many special advantages but raises great difficulties in cost, adaptability, and continuity with present form.

Of course, these are all "pure" types that make no concessions to the complications of reality and they have been described as though they were states of perfection to be maintained forever. In actuality, a plan for a metropolis is more likely to be a complex and mixed one, to be realized as an episode in some continuous process, whose form involves rate and direction of change as well as a momentary pattern.

For example, let us consider, on the basis of the little we know, a form that might better satisfy our aspirations, if we accept the fact of metropolitan agglomeration: this form is in essence a variant of the dispersed urban sheet. Imagine a metropolis in which the flow system becomes more specialized and complex, assuming a triangular grid pattern that grows at the edges and becomes more specialized in the interior. Many types of flow would be provided for. Densities would have a wide range and a fine grain, with intensive peaks at junctions in the circulation system and with linear concentrations along major channels, but with extensive regions of low density inside the grid. Through the interstices of this network belts and tongues of open land would form another kind of grid. Thus the general pattern would resemble a fisherman's net, with a system of dispersed centers and intervening spaces.

City-wide activities would concentrate in these knots of density, which would be graded in size. In the smaller centers the activities would not be specialized, but the larger centers would be increasingly dominated by some special activity. Therefore the major centers would be highly specialized— although never completely "pure"—and would be arranged in a loose central cluster, each highly accessible.

A metropolis of twenty million might have, not one such

cluster, but two or three whose spheres of influence would overlap. These clusters might be so dense as to be served by transportation grids organized in three dimensions, like a skeletal framework in space. Elsewhere, the network would thin out and adapt itself to local configurations of topography.

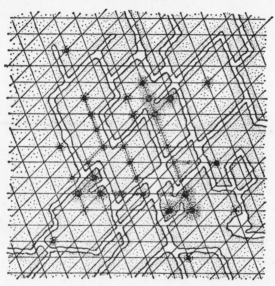

Fig. 9. The Multicentered Net.

This general pattern would continue to specialize and to grow, perhaps in a rhythmically pulsating fashion. With growth and decay, parts of the whole would undergo periodic renewal. Such a form might satisfy many of the general criteria, but each particular metropolis is likely to encounter special problems. Even so, the description illustrates the complexity, the indeterminacy, and the dynamic nature of city form that are inherent in any such generalization.

Perhaps we can make such a proposal more concrete by stating it as a set of actions rather than as a static pattern. If this were the form desired, then the agencies of control would adopt certain definite policies. First, they would encourage continued metropolitan agglomeration. Second, they would begin to construct a generalized triangular grid of channels for transportation, adapting its interspacing and alignment to circumstances, but aiming at raising accessibility throughout the area as a whole. This grid would provide for many different kinds of flow and would have a hierarchy of its own—that is, the lines of circulation would be differentiated with respect to the intensity and speed of their traffic. Third, peaks of activity and density would be encouraged, but in sharply defined areas, not in rings whose density gradually declines from the center. The present metropolitan center would be encouraged to specialize and thus loosen into a cluster, while one or two major rival centers might develop elsewhere in the network, rather than allowing a general dispersal of city-wide activities. Such major specialized centers might be given even greater local intensity, with multi-level circulation, perhaps as a three-dimensional system of public rights-of-way.

Fourth, every effort would be made to retain, acquire, or clear a system of linked open spaces of generous size that pervaded the network. Fifth, a wide variety of activities, of accommodation, and of structural character, dispersed in a fine-grained pattern, would be encouraged. Once the concentration of special activities and the arrangement of higher densities in centers and along major channels had been provided for, then zoning and other controls would be employed only to maintain the minimum grain needed to preserve the character and efficiency of the various types of use and density, and large single-purpose areas would be avoided. Sixth, the form of centers, transportation channels, and major open spaces would be controlled so as to give as vivid a visual image as possible. Seventh, the agency would be committed to continuous rebuilding and reorganization of successive parts of the pattern.

Such a set of policies would mean a radical redirection of metropolitan growth. Whether this plan is feasible or worth the cost would require serious consideration. Even if this pattern were chosen, there would still be many crucial questions of relative emphasis and timing to be weighed. If life in the future metropolis is to be worthy of the massive effort necessary to build it, the physical pattern must satisfy human values. The coordination of metropolitan development, however obligatory, will not of itself ensure this happy result. Coordination must be directed toward some desired general pattern, and, to define this, we must clarify our alternatives and the goals they are meant to serve.

REFERENCES

1. Frank Lloyd Wright, "Broadacre City," in *Taliesin,* October 1940, vol. 1, no. 1.
2. Clarence Stein, "City Patterns, Past and Future," *Pencil Points,* June 1942.
3. *Skitseforslag tol egnsplan for Storkobenhaven:* Copenhagen regional plan. Summary of the preliminary proposal, 1948-1949, with list of contents and notes explaining all illustrations of the preliminary proposal, translated into English.
4. Hans Blumenfeld, "A Theory of City Form," *Society of Architectural Historians Journal,* July 1949.

7. On Social Communication and the Metropolis

KARL W. DEUTSCH

ANY METROPOLIS CAN be thought of as a huge engine of communication, a device to enlarge the range and reduce the cost of individual and social choices. In the familiar telephone switchboard, the choices consist of many different lines. Plugging in the wires to connect any two lines is an act of commitment, since it implies foregoing the making of other connections. The concentration of available outlets on the switchboard permits a wider range of alternative choices than would prevail under any more dispersed arrangement. It also imposes less stringent conditions of compatibility. The limits for the potentially useful size of a switchboard are fixed by the capacity of the type of switching and control equipment available.

The facilities of the metropolis for transport and communication are the equivalent of the switchboard. The units of commitment are not necessarily telephone calls but more often face-to-face meetings and transactions. For any participant to enter into any one transaction usually will exclude other transactions. Every transaction thus implies a commitment. The facilities available for making choices and commitments will then limit the useful size of a metropolis.

CONTACT CHOICES: THE PRODUCT OF CITIES

From this perspective, the performance of a metropolis could be measured in terms of the average number of contact choices which it offers to its inhabitants within, say, one hour of round-trip commuting time, at the prevailing levels of effort and equipment.[1] Efficiency in cities, as in other organizations, differs from effectiveness. Effectiveness is the probability of carrying out a given type of performance, regardless of cost, while efficiency consists in low cost for a given performance. The more persons or services available to a city dweller within a round trip of one hour, the more effective would be his city or metropolitan area, and the cheaper the cost of maintaining a metropolis area; and the cheaper the cost of maintaining a metropolis that places, say 1,000,000 people and 50,000 public and private institutions, firms, or service points within a given commuting radius, the more efficient the metropolis could be said to be. The effectiveness of a metropolis could be measured in contact choices within one hour of travel time, while the efficiency of the same city would be measured by the ratio of such choices to some unit of cost. How many choices will $100 per capita buy for the residents of city X? As in many problems of design, one criterion cannot entirely override another. Some increases in effectiveness may have to be sought even at the price of rising costs, and some gains in efficiency may be worth some concessions in performance.

According to this view, the essential performance of the metropolis is in the enhancement of the range and number of such choices, and the basic cost is the maintenance of a system of facilities that makes a wide range of choices possible. One might ask: how many choices can an individual buy at a cost he can afford—and how many such choices on the average can the community buy for different groups of people, at prices it can afford? For each type of city and for each type of communication and transport system, it might then be possible to sketch demand and cost curves based either on the best available knowledge, or on prevailing practice.

Large cities, of course, serve many other functions. They offer playgrounds for children, lanes for lovers, shelter for residents and transients. But houses, playgrounds, and lovers' lanes are found in villages as well, and so sometimes are factories, power stations and mills, as well as manor houses and castles. Almost any one kind of installation found in a metropolis can also be found in the countryside. It is the multiplicity of different facilities and of persons, and the wide choice of potential quick contacts among them, that makes the metropolis what it is. And this essential character applies to large cities in underdeveloped as well as in advanced countries.

This general function of the metropolis is facilitated by its geographic location at some nodal point in a larger transportation network. The more the arteries that intersect at the site of the city, the greater the opportunities the city has to facilitate a wide range of choice. Again, the larger the city, the more diversified its industries, repair shops, and service installations —hospitals, research institutes, libraries, and labor exchanges— the wider the range of possible choices among them. The larger, the more diversified, the more highly skilled and educated the population, the greater the range of available personal choice either with respect to organizations or to opportunities in the world of culture, recreation, and the arts.

In terms of economics, particularly in regard to the location of industrial enterprises, many of these considerations appear as external economies, actual or expected. Roads, port and rail connections, municipal services, the supply of skilled and unskilled labor, and the availability of high-level professional and scientific talent—all appear as so many potential factors of production, and some of them may even appear as free goods, against which no additional items of cost need to be budgeted. As will be evident later, the expectation may not be an altogether realistic one: the effective attractions of the area for new industries may lead after a time lag of some years or decades to substantial problems of congestion and overload. Yet locating in or near a great city is not only an exercise in economic rationality. Often the decision is made in intuitive and human terms; and most often perhaps the economic reasoning and the human preferences for location may seem to rein-

force one another. Both tend to seek a widening range of
choice at low, or at least tolerable, costs of choosing; and just
this is the special advantage of the city. The rising proportions
of industrial staff whose jobs are oriented to communication,
service, or professional functions may reinforce this attraction.

The power of the metropolis as an engine of communication
is thus attested indirectly by its power of attraction over
people. Though this power has an economic component, in the
aggregate it is far more than economic. "How ya gonna keep
'em down on the farm, after they've seen Paree?" asked an old
song; and the sociologists and anthropologists of the 1940's
and 1950's have been reporting the vast attraction of urban
areas in Asia and Africa to former villagers, far beyond any
immediate economic or social push. They are held even in
the squalor of the shanty towns and *bidonvilles.* If freedom is
the opportunity to choose, then the metropolis, in so far as it
is an engine for facilitating choice, is also an engine of liberation. This liberation may be physical, in terms of the visits, the
meetings, the sights now possible, or it may be psychological
and vicarious, in terms of the choices and experiences which
can now be made in the imagination. In either case, it is a
liberation whose reality and whose social, political, and psychological relevance cannot be doubted.

COMMUNICATION OVERLOAD:
THE DISEASE OF CITIES

People come to large cities because there, among other
reasons, they find a wider range of choice within their individual limitations than they are likely to find anywhere else. Inevitably this means that every metropolis must offer each of its
residents enough freedom for a wide range of choices to be
significant to him; and this also means enough freedom so
that serious problems of peak loads and of recurrent, possibly
growing, overloads are imposed on the city's many but limited
facilities. Recurrent overloads are thus not an alien disturbance

intruding into the even functioning of the metropolis. They are, on the contrary, an ever possible result of the essential nature of the metropolis as a device for facilitating a wider range of free choices.

To put it differently, the likelihood of such overloads is a result of the probability of coincidences in human choices and behavior under conditions of freedom. These overloads are not only the occasional loads, for which reserve capacities must be provided, but also the regular rush-hour loads, the result of relatively synchronized hours for work and recreation which in turn permit a larger range of choices than staggered hours would.

Despite their origin, however, recurrent overloads will tend to paralyze many functions, and eventually to blight the very structure of a metropolis. It is for good reason that waiting-line theory has become a fast-growing field in operations research and social science. Taken together, increasing overloads of this kind reduce or destroy many attractions of the metropolis as well as the economic value of many of the capital investments in it.

Even in the absence of such overloads, the very effectiveness of a metropolis may produce subtle changes in its culture and in the cast of mind of its residents. A wider range of relevant choices implies ordinarily an additional burden on those who are choosing. Some years ago, Clifton Fadiman wrote a thoughtful article, "The Decline of Attention" in modern, and especially American, culture.[2] Since then Richard Meier has written of "attention overload" and of the "communication-saturated" society as characteristic problems of modern—and thus particularly of urban and metropolitan—culture.[3] These, too, are overloads in communication, but they occur not in streets and telephone lines but within the minds and nervous systems of people.

To increase the range of visible and relevant choices that confront a person usually means to increase the opportunity cost of whatever course he may eventually choose. Whatever he does will necessarily imply foregoing something else that also has appeared relevant and in a sense attractive. The wider the range of relevant choices we put before a person of limited physical and psychic resources and capabilities, the more acute and pressing we make his problem of economy in allocating his own time, attention, and resources; and if he has been raised in a "conscientious" culture, such as the American or Northwest European, we are quite likely also to have increased his vague but nagging sense of self-doubt and misgiving as to whether he had made the best choice, and thus the best use, of his opportunities.

Cities therefore may produce a pervasive condition of communications overload. Whereas villagers thirst for gossip, city dwellers with more ample choices may crave privacy. But the internal communications overload of other people makes them less receptive to our needs. Their limited attention or their real need for privacy may tend to exclude us, and in the midst of crowds of neighbors we may experience persistent loneliness. Such loneliness, inflicted on us by others, is the obverse of our own need for privacy; and our own limited capabilities for concentration, attention, and responsiveness will make both their and our loneliness less likely to be overcome.

What people cannot overcome, they may try to gloss over. The poets and the social scientists—both critics of our culture —have catalogued the many rituals of self-deception that men practice: the reading of mass media that purvey illusions of "inside information" to the millions commonly excluded from it; the fancy dress of conformity which they don, from Ivy-League dress to the black leather jackets of youth gangs, or beatnik beards and sandals. Even these foibles that convey a sense of belonging, of identity, should be seen in perspective. People indulge in them, not necessarily because they are more shallow or stupid than their forebears in a village or small town, but because the commitments the metropolis imposes— of greater freedom, wider choices, greater burdens on their attentions and their powers of response—have temporarily become too much for them.

This temporary overburdening may be particularly acute for newcomers from some radically different cultural background. Then the effects of psychological uprooting through contact with the wider opportunities of metropolitan life are superimposed on the effects of the shock of a new culture and the weakening of the traditional bonds of family and familiar authority.

Communication overloads may be reduced through effective cues for orientation. Consider, for example, the practice of the old city builders, who placed the most important structures of visual attraction, such as cathedrals, palaces, or monuments, at the nodal points in the street network of the city. The nodal points, as the term is used here, were those located at the main intersections of the city's traffic flow, and hence most often observed as the city's landmarks, and they were also those points most useful for orientation. The experience of visual beauty in a place of visual usefulness was thus often an inevitable part of a city dweller's daily coming and going. It is perhaps not too fanciful to surmise that this combined experience of perception and clarity of orientation in such cities as London, Paris, Bern, Cologne, or Prague contributed, and still contributes, to the charm of those cities and to the feeling of their inhabitants that they were members of a deep and rich culture. Bridges can fulfil a similar orienting function: the San Francisco Bay Bridge and the Golden Gate Bridge come readily to mind, together with the Embarcadero Tower of the old ferry building, visible for a long distance along the major artery of Market Street.

In many modern metropolitan areas, however, these conditions are no longer fulfilled. Major intersections in many American cities are often adorned with gasoline stations or car lots, with flimsy, low shop buildings with large neon signs. At the same time, many of the largest, most expensive, and sometimes most impressive constructions are put on side lots, well away from the main intersections, as for example Rockefeller Center, the Lever and Seagram buildings, the United Nations building, or the Museum of Modern Art, in New York City. In

Boston, the John Hancock building, tallest and most monumental in the city, is tucked away on a side street.[4] Many of
our visible landmarks are only of very limited help in orientation, and are best seen from afar or by special visit. At the
same time, many of the major intersections passed daily by
most of us are either nondescript or appallingly ugly and give
subtle but depressing impressions of disorientation, tiredness,
or tension.

Such crucial traffic points cannot be easily abandoned. When
elegant entertainment and shopping shifted from the central
intersection of Times Square to the area of Rockefeller Center,
the old subway system became less convenient to users of the
Center, who have to make their way there and back by foot,
bus, or taxi, and who thus have increased congestion. This contrast between the changing fashions in regard to neighborhoods and the unchanging nature of fixed intersections in a
major traffic network helps to make the market mechanism
such an unsatisfactory instrument for the development of these
crucial sites.[5]

Overloads on some of the public and private services available in an urban area may sometimes be reinforced in their
effects by a shrinking, or even an atrophy, of these services.
Services vulnerable to this kind of process include service and
repair shops, stockrooms, and parts depots, hospitals and
clinics, libraries and museums. Many of the services of these
institutions might be needed on Saturdays, in some cases, as is
true of the cultural institutions, or on Sundays, or often for
many hours on each work day. Institutions such as supermarkets and suburban shopping centers provide such longer
hours of service, but many others do not, and some now curtail
the amount of service previously offered. Much of this situation seems caused by rising labor costs, by fixed budgets, by
the rising cost of able managers for small or middle-sized
undertakings, or by the difficulty of dividing units of managerial effort so as to obtain management for some extra hours
daily or weekly, and perhaps by some subtle development in

American metropolitan areas that makes the personnel in service industries prefer shorter hours to more pay. This may be a rational choice, but it may become less so if too much of the new leisure is frittered away in waiting for delayed services. An increase in staff, with additional compensation for staggered hours (already practiced in suburban supermarkets), might be one approach an affluent society could well explore. In any case, free-market forces alone seem unlikely to overcome the persistent gap between the rising need for services in metropolitan areas and the actual volume of services rendered.

SUBURBS: AN ESCAPE FROM OVERLOADS

In the congested metropolis, a major effect of the cumulative overloads on communications, transport, and other urban amenities is frustration. Withdrawal to a suburb offers partial surcease. Taxes play a role in these frustrations. The late Justice Holmes once said he did not mind paying taxes, for this was the way he bought civilization; but exasperated city dwellers may flee to the suburbs from a metropolis where so much tax money buys so little in civilized living. The remedy is not to lower the urban tax cost as such but to improve the quality of metropolitan government and metropolitan living by attacking the whole range of overloads. Several lines for such an attack have been proposed, but most are proposals for escape. When put into practice they have not been markedly successful. For example, the shift in population to dormitory suburbs around the old cities has produced mounting burdens on commuting. A farther shift to some twenty-five or fifty miles from the city would make commuting prohibitive for many; and, whereas some men have been able to afford the financial and physical costs, their wives have found themselves marooned in a more or less rural environment, deprived of most of the choices and opportunities that make city life attractive.

The schemes for satellite towns are more far-reaching: each

would be near the city, with separate though limited facilities
for employment, shopping, services, and entertainment. Some
towns of this kind have been built, but in Britain, at least, they
have proved less popular than expected.[6] Still more far-
reaching schemes for decentralization would break up the
large cities altogether in favor of a wide scattering of major
factories and administrative offices over much greater regions.
Such a proposal would require a heavy reliance on medium-
and long-distance transport and on telecommunications, as
well as the acceptance of rural (or nearly rural) isolation.

All these schemes are unsatisfactory in the same fundamental respect. For escape from the frustrations of the metropolis,
they would sacrifice the primary purpose of the large city—a
wider range of choice with a low cost. The search for more
effective ways of dealing with urban problems cannot ignore
this basic function of a metropolis; rather this must be the starting point.

A STRATEGY OF SEARCH FOR SOLUTIONS

The concept of a metropolis as a device for facilitating choice
in communications can contribute first of all to answering some
general questions, from which one may proceed to more
specific surmises and to ways in which both the tentative general answers and the specific surmises can be tested. The first
questions might be these: What is the usual ratio of the cost
of transport and communication facilities to the cost of shelter?
How does this ratio change for different types of cities? How is
it influenced by an increase in the scale of a city, as measured
by its total population?

There are several ways of exploring this inquiry; they should
give us interchangeable indices of the same underlying fact.[7]
The proportion of communication costs to shelter costs could
be measured in terms of the ratio of total capital investment in
communication and transport facilities to the total capital investment in shelter. Or it could be measured in terms of the

ratio of current expenditure of communication and transport to current expenditure on shelter; or in terms of the ratio of total manpower employed in communication and transport to the manpower employed in the construction and maintenance of shelter. Doubtless, a range of further indicators of this kind for related ratios might be developed, but those already given should serve amply to illustrate the point.

One could also study the ratios of some appropriate non-monetary indicators, such as the physical proportions of certain relevant facilities. The known ratio of the area of land that is devoted to streets in a city to the land area devoted to dwellings and gardens could perhaps be used more effectively within the context of the other ratios noted above.

Other types of large-scale organization could be studied. As taller skyscrapers are built, what is the change in the ratio of space devoted to elevator shafts to the total volume of the building? As corporations grow bigger, what is the ratio of telephone calls and written messages to some measure of the total volume of company activities? Such questions are aimed not merely at promoting speculation but also at suggesting a surmise to be tested: as the size and functions of a city grow, the proportion of resources devoted to transport and communications may have to grow faster, or at least as fast, if increasing overloads are to be avoided. It may be that some lag may produce no ill effects. Then the crucial question would be: What lag in the growth of such facilities is acceptable? Research may disclose a range of acceptable or desirable proportions for investment in such facilities and thus offer a potentially useful tool to planners.

What would life be like in an otherwise normal metropolis if its transport and communication facilities had been deliberately somewhat overdeveloped by present-day standards? Suppose its streets and intersections were hardly ever jammed, its parking spaces rarely unavailable, its public transport frequent, rapid, clean, and uncrowded, its telephone lines usually free, with quickly available connections? If this sounds too much like utopia, it might still be asked: How much improvement in well-being in a city could be purchased by how large an investment in drastically improved transport and communication?

Some years ago, Sigfried Giedion drew attention to the late-nineteenth-century shift to the pavilion system in large exhibitions, away from the earlier practice of centralizing all major exhibits in one giant building of the Crystal Palace type.[8] Giedion suggested that, as the exhibitions and the crowds of visitors grew larger, they gave rise to intolerable demands for more corridors to keep the crowds moving. The solution devised was to break up the exhibition into scattered pavilions, and to let the visitors make their way from one to another across the network of footpaths or across the open ground. People preferred to walk hundreds of yards in the open to the next pavilion rather than push their way for dozens of yards along some crowded corridor or hall. The principle may be relevant perhaps to the metropolis and the problems of urban decentralization.

Again, the question of cost arises. The shift to the pavilion system made the visitors themselves responsible for keeping dry and warm, a cost previously borne by the management of the single central hall. When a shift occurs from a compact city to a spreading network of suburbs, costs are also shifted from the city government to suburban families, who must now maintain one or two cars and pay toll rates for most of their telephone calls. In addition, there is now the financial, physical, and nervous cost of commuting. The decisive factor is the increase in delay in arriving and in the danger and tension. The ten or twelve miles between Wellesley and Boston may require twenty-five to thirty minutes with light traffic and good weather, in bad weather or dense traffic, forty-five minutes or more; and there are perhaps a hundred intersections. Over an adequate expressway the same trip might take fifteen to twenty minutes, with less tension and fatigue. A radial and peripheral system of improved expressways, permitting safe traveling speeds of seventy miles an hour—assuming corresponding improvements in the safety features of cars—would permit a city to double its effective radius and quadruple its potential area of integration. Our road experts have told us that "speed kills" if resorted to at the wrong time and place. But our city planners might well remind us that delays, too, can kill when their cumulative burden is added over a long period to an intensive working day.

Safe speed is not cheap. It cannot be achieved except by planned investment under public guidance. But it could do much to humanize life in our cities. The day may come when a profession of specialized expediters may watch over the smooth and quick flow of traffic and communication in our metropolitan areas, to identify and remove bottlenecks and overloads before their effects become cumulative and choking.

The same considerations apply even more strongly to public transportation. Improved and publicly subsidized rail transport—on the ground and underground—offers perhaps some of the most promising opportunities to combine high speed in mass transportation with safety at tolerable cost. The old-style commuting trains that take forty minutes for twenty miles not only exhaust their passengers but also drive more and more people to the somewhat faster highways. A drastic improvement in the speed and caliber of public transportation might relieve the pressure on the road system. Similarly, an extension of local telephone call rates to the entire suburban area—on the analogy of the successful principle of uniform postal rates—might reduce some of the need to travel back and forth and thus further reduce the pressure on the transport system. Still another step might be the partial staggering of service hours, so that more stores and service facilities would be available for more hours daily, thus reducing the peak loads when all stores open or close. Rotating assignments and staggered hours might require more employees, but it might pay off in higher profits for the stores and in greater freedom for the community.[9]

None of these improvements would be cheap, and none easy

to achieve. Such improvements, however, might be a key factor in rehabilitating our metropolitan areas. What is needed is a realistic analysis of the problem of peak loads and of the rising capital requirements for transport and communication. Only a substantial investment in transportation and communications can make metropolitan decentralization practicable, and only a substantial strengthening of public control over strategic land sites can restore beauty to our cities. Ways will have to be found to let planners use the powers of the community to guide urban growth toward a clear and pleasing pattern of new and old landmarks where people can once again feel well-oriented, exhilarated, and at home.

The various lines of research suggested in these pages have a common origin and a common goal. Our inquiry has centered on the function of a metropolis in aiding its residents in their choices and in their search for responses. The ranges and costs of such choices and responses are basic to our analysis. Proportionately accelerated investment in communications, together with an improved knowledge of the general order of magnitude of these proportions, suggests a possible approach to urban decentralization. It also points up the need for greater clarity and beauty in our cities, and perhaps also for more responsive government, capable of integrating a wider range of metropolitan and suburban services, if the expanded metropolis is to become a genuine home for its people.

REFERENCES

1. This would be analogous to measuring the performance of a switchboard or of a central telephone exchange in terms of the number of potential calls among which an average subscriber might be able to choose, say, for ten cents, or within thirty seconds' time for dialing, automatic switching, signaling, and the first response of the called party.
2. Clifton Fadiman, "The Decline of Attention," in *The Saturday Review Reader* (New York: Bantam Books, 1951), pp. 25-36.
3. I am indebted for the term to Richard L. Meier; see his "Characteristics of the New Urbanization" (multigraphed, University of Chicago, 1953), especially pp. 3-5.
4. There are exceptions in many cities, to be sure. The Prudential Building in Chicago, the Coliseum Exhibition Hall at Columbus Circle in New York, and the Liberty Mutual Building in Boston are all at major intersections. These seem to have been exceptions, however, so far as major post-1930 construction is concerned.
5. Many users of the new facilities have employed a new transport system—the taxicab—but the cost to the community includes not only the cab fare but also the surface traffic jams and perhaps the exclusion of a marginal class of customers for the new facilities.
6. Lloyd Rodwin, *The British New Towns Policy* (Cambridge: Harvard University Press, 1941).
7. See Paul F. Lazarsfeld's discussion on the interchangeability of indices in his article, "Evidence and Inference in Social Research," *Dædalus,* 1958, no. 4, pp. 99-130 (*On Evidence and Inference*).
8. Sigfried Giedion, *Space, Time and Architecture* (Cambridge: Harvard University Press, 1941), pp. 262, n-11, 725-727, 736-742, 757.
9. For a discussion of some limiting factors and of the forces tending to pull the working hours of the whole community into a single rhythm, see Vilhelm Aubert and Harrison White, "Sleep: A Sociological Interpretation," *Acta Sociologica,* 1960, *4:* no. 3, 1-16.

8. The Changing Uses of the City

JOHN DYCKMAN

INTRODUCTION: FORCES INFLUENCING THE CHANGING CITY

THERE IS SOME evidence that men took to the city slowly. The early cities of Eastern culture were built by villagers as sacred centers for religious or ritual retreat. Eventually, the villager moved into the city with the concentration of agricultural surplus, the extended specialization of consumption, the assembly of a labor pool, and the growing economies of scale and social overhead as the urbanites developed technology. Thereafter, the momentum of urbanization took over on its own, freed for action by facilitating noneconomic institutions. Today, when the old economies of the city are dwindling in importance in the wealthiest industrial countries, metropolitan growth rushes on. But the urbanites, some of whom remain in village-like pockets in the hearts of the cities, show signs of resuming the village roots in the new suburbia.

Bertrand Russell once observed, in comment on Lloyd Morgan's optimistic doctrine of emergent evolution, "If indeed the world in which we live has been produced in accordance with a Plan, we shall have to reckon Nero a Saint in comparison with the Author of that Plan." Our emerging metropolitan civilization at times inspires similar sentiments in the hearts of its would-be planners. But if our cities have been produced by neither human nor divine plan, they are nonetheless a faithful mirror of our culture.

144

In contemporary America, the forces exerting the greatest influence on the changing city are so pervasive they sometimes escape attention. Among them we should surely include:

1. The late-industrial technology, fed by the rapid leaps of modern science rather than the old painfully wrought steps of the industrial arts.

2. The ubiquitous growth of socio-economic *organization*, manifest in the form of

    a. continuation of the long-time trend to "bigness";

    b. extension of process of specialization, with its interdependence and hierarchical ordering of parts;

    c. development of a self-conscious management rationale and an embryonic theory and science of organization.

3. In the advanced industrial economies, the early signs of the first appearance of a sufficiently large societal surplus to permit the widespread weakening of old economic drives and motivation (this development has thus far been disguised by noneconomic military priorities).

4. A rapid leap in communication facilities and the subsequent growth of world-wide communication (including the upsurge in literacy and shared symbols) which has made the world functionally "smaller" and has raised the potential for changing old boundaries and old definitions of community.

5. The deepening awareness of cultural impoverishment relative to American material prosperity. The task of raising mass culture above the levels of its present vulgarity is inseparable from the awakening of mass interest in public canons of consumption. Respect for the communal arts and public services is a prerequisite for the development of public tastes. So far this awareness is confined to intellectuals, but with the aid of communication resources at their command, they may bring it to broader public attention.

One would wish to add a sixth force, that of a rising concern with organized city planning, but the evidence for it is not yet strong.

These developments are so closely interwoven that it is impossible to separate their contributions to the changing physical form and the changing cultural image of the city. Nonetheless, we shall indulge in some speculation about their individual and combined impact on the urban innovations ahead.

LATE INDUSTRIAL TECHNOLOGY AND
THE PHYSICAL CITY

In the early stages of the evolution of the city, industrialization, though only one of many social changes, was the decisive one. Without it the metropolis would have been impossible; without it the metropolis would have been unnecessary. The city, in turn, was an important artifact in the creation of an industrial civilization. Now, however, the marriage faces possible dissolution. For one thing, industry is freer than it has ever been to set up outside the city. For another, both the "city" and "industry" are less clearly defined. The former has been submerged in a tide of urbanization which does not respect clear-cut boundaries. The latter has evolved from recognizable processes of shaping and fabricating materials to a range of activities shading almost imperceptibly in some cases from pure science to manipulation of human motives. The change from the technology of steam, coal, and iron to electric power has not produced the dirt-free, decentralized city of the Geddes-Mumford[1] dream, but there are few now who would feel it to be impossible. Newer power sources, most notably solar energy, may carry out the job which the gasoline engine has crudely and imperfectly begun.[2]

These developments, of course, will be applied, if they are applied, at first only on the margins. Like progressive education, they will be debated and even superseded long before they have received widespread application. And in the meantime, our cities continue to feel the full impact of the older technology and still reap the whirlwind of its transformation of an agricultural society. Living with this heritage, the contemporary city dweller hopes to escape from the uglier by-products, or waits for "renewal." It is hard for him to see anything in his organizational role that is helping to bring about new living forms which will be free of the mills that usurp the river banks and pollute the lakes, the congestion that burns up a cloud of smog, and the waves of rural workers moving into a chaos of residential decay. But if the city still means excitement, ideas, and license to him, he will not—in the absence of suitable alternatives—want to be far away from it, either. This is the limbo in which the half-empowered city dweller of today finds himself, and the halfway solutions which he seeks in suburbia are familiar to all.

TECHNOLOGY AND POPULATION DISTRIBUTION

Cheaper, faster transport is potentially decentralizing (and given the same population, density reducing) since it permits workers to achieve the same real costs of travel to work at greater distance from the job. When an improvement of transport technology cuts the costs of assembly and distribution significantly, it may reduce pressure to achieve economies by a particular location, that is, it may leave the activity less space-tied. On the other hand, engineering improvements in site utilization (for example, storage capacity) increase the ability of a site to provide services at a given transport cost, and so may have a potentially centralizing effect.

Thus in a rapidly changing technology conditions are being created which may make both higher densities and lower densities more economic. Since technological innovations are themselves selected by economic factors, however, consumer demand plays a part in making its own bed. The dispersal attained with the relatively costly auto commutation is an indicator of the direction in which that demand leans. Decentralization trends may be boosted further by the exhaustion of the fossil fuels such as coal and petroleum, and their replacement by the direct utilization of solar energy.[3] The amount of space required per unit, the freedom of units from fixed power sources, and the requisite spacing of units indicate a relatively low density of development for residences using this type of energy.

The use of atomic power may serve to postpone this decentralization. The economic size of an atomic power plant is currently very large, and while the plant itself should not, for obvious reasons, be located in the heart of a major population center, it can most efficiently serve a large, concentrated market at some point nearby. Strides in the improvement of space-utilization in buildings are also possible, thus permitting the more intensive use of space "at the center of things." Microfilm, magnetic tapes, transistors, and other devices are achieving this effect in many kinds of data storage essential to business. In a much smaller way, urban renewal has worked to this end in the residential sector by replacing large but inefficient units with smaller and more "functional" ones. Measured in terms of the volume of activity taking place at a given point, rather than by the persons assembled, the capacity of land in our central places has been increased enormously in recent years, though this change has been disguised in central office districts by a more lavish use of space.

At the same time, individuals are less rooted to any one place. With more free time and more income in his hands, the individual's travel costs become relatively smaller. The range of activities within his grasp becomes larger. Under these circumstances, it is not unlikely that the extent and variety of spaces "consumed" by the individual should increase, and that his use of space should become more functionally specialized. This has long been an observable characteristic of the well-to-do, some of whom keep a separate apartment or house for such diverse functions as dwelling, work, theater-going, duck-shooting, and winter and summer vacationing. On a more significant scale, a limited variant of this kind of special-purpose use of place and structure might be made available to large numbers of persons with technological developments which would make both the individual units and the travel to reach them cheaper.

A nondiscriminating technology, making possible both greater centralization and greater decentralization, might be turned to both uses simultaneously by a wealthy, pragmatic nation. One possible outcome is a kind of permanent oscillation between the dense city center and the sparsely settled outer suburbia; between a tiny but well-equipped cubicle (one-upping the "beats," a super-functional "pad") and a virtually portable solar-powered house. If the style of life of the multitudes who are electing to live in Southern California at the rate of a thousand a day is symptomatic of a deep American wish, provisions ought also to be made for long periods of living in a boat or trailer.

CENTRALIZATION, DECENTRALIZATION, AND DENSITY

Density of settlement and the spacing of persons, according to persistent beliefs, materially affect the quality of life. In the early industrial era, when the close quarters of the industrial towns were accompanied by bad diet, poor sanitary engineering, little knowledge of the transmission of disease, and the low immunity to these hazards of a recently rural labor force, the rapid increase of urban density nearly proved a total disaster. In the later stages of the growth of the city, density has acquired a connotation of urbanity, and has thereby come to be associated with social development and intellectual awareness. Especially when contrasted with a peasant countryside, the city has been championed as the natural habitat of learning and the richest soil for cultural flowering.

It is no longer appropriate to associate high density with plagues, but it may be equally ill-fitting to correlate low density with "the idiocy of the countryside." The distinctions between city and country are in need of revision to fit the realities of present possibilities. Further, the vices and virtues attributed to the city were never wholly assignable to density *per se*. We still know little of the safely realizable densities of human congregation and of their effects on human performance.

Biological populations seem to show some "critical mass" beyond which the individual, as well as the group, exhibits malfunction and breakdown. The National Institute of Mental Health, in its researches, has shown a disposition to attempt to extend the findings on various animal populations to human groups by analogy. While human groups need not suffer as a group from being of a size that presses on a local food supply (at least in United States society), one suspects the existence of some more subtle stresses on the individual under certain conditions. Support for this view is supplied indirectly by recent biological research on the causes of disease and mass "neuroses" in rodents.[4]

At the same time, there is evidence of strong congregating tendencies in human populations, including a tendency to congestion even where space is available, free, and riskless.[5] The possibilities for an efficient storage of information and activity, and so for greater concentrations of persons, are implicit in much of our new communications technology, which tends to be "space" as well as "weight-losing." Given the trends in world urbanization, one does not need a concept of "pathological togetherness"[6] to suggest that we will have much greater massing in future cities than in the present.

Will we then find a way to adjust our rhythm of life to swing gracefully between dense massings and lonely retreat? If this chameleon society should develop, constantly adjusting "tension gates" might need to be developed as part of man's psychosomatic regulation, permitting him to raise or lower the bars to reception of stimuli under dramatically different environmental conditions.

CITIZENS OF A CHANGING CITY

The present effort at urban renewal may, in the long view, appear as the last-ditch attempt to save the old form of the city and the style of life it supported. Paradoxically, the mobilized corporate effort necessary for the large changes has in this instance been devoted to the braking of change. The individuals in the market, voting with their dollars and their feet, have shown little of this nostalgia for the old forms. What is more, the people who show the greatest enthusiasm for the new forms of urban living—the suburban and exurban varieties —are drawn from the ranks of the conformist, security-oriented "organization men." This suggests that there is a covert understanding that the dominant corporate image is favorable to the new forms, despite a token allegiance to the old city.

The visible changes in the city may suggest a deeper social change than has actually taken place. Middle-class Americans take their style of life with them, with only minor alterations, through various zones of suburbia. The heralded changes in the political affiliations of city workers which were expected to attend their increasing moves to mass suburbia and home ownership have been small. No doubt differences in the superficial aspects of culture, in the traditional symbols of class, nationality, or ethnic group, are reduced in the suburban resettlement of old working-class neighborhoods. But these changes are small compared with those still being experienced by rural in-migrants entering the oldest sectors of the city.

Both these movements, by reducing the backlog of differences, diminish the potential for future change. The long march of the under-employed rural labor force to the city, when seen through the glass of the once proud middle-class neighborhoods in its path, appears precipitate and devastating. It must be remembered, however, that these are the last throes of the change. The new urban recruits are being drawn from the most culturally remote areas, long bypassed. These laborers in the vineyard will be the last, barring open-door immigration, for whom the move to the city will be a great cultural, social, and economic leap.

At the same time as the last pockets of rural isolation are being rooted out and incorporated into the disciplined organization of urban society, that organization is changing its rules of enlistment. The transition from an industrial to a "techno-

logical" organization has altered the requirements for education, social recruitment, and class distinctions, has changed the
meaning of work, has robbed leisure of its release, and cloaked
status in more obscure symbols.

The migrant from the subsistence economy of the hills
always found it difficult to adjust to the industrial discipline of
the factory system. Now that work is further depersonalized,
the relation of worker to output less apparent, individual
craftsmanship less applicable, and control more remote, the
personal impact of the change is staggering. Neither the independence of the mountain man nor the social cohesion of the
Puerto Rican villager is a usable resource in this new situation.

Even the children of veteran urbanites, the wise young of
the cities, find important sources of meaningful activity drain-
ing away, as some novelist-critics have underlined.[7] The
elaboration of the uses of the automobile, along with hi-fi,
boats, etc., is not only a cultivation of the garden of craftsmanship in a desert of routine, but serves even more importantly
to give the user a power over the environment which is otherwise denied him even in his work. One need only to look to the
developing economies of Asia, Africa, and Latin America to
see that it is the promise of self-determination contained in
technology, not the exercise of a new craft, that beguiles them.

ALIENATION IN THE CITY

The greater separation of the place of residence from the
place of work (a hallmark of the modern city) accentuates the
separation of man from his productive activity. In space as
well as in function, his leisure is freed from the taint of work
(the exceptions are the activities of some writers, advertisers,
salesmen, and communications executives, whose work is
wrapped around the exploitation of others' leisure). Efforts to
re-establish contact through "do-it-yourself" projects are not
convincing.

Atomized leisure activities have failed to fuse into any satisfying esthetic of consumption. As Riesman has pointed out, conspicuous consumption (which bequeathed us many of our contemporary antiques and much of the monumental architecture and urban sculpture so revered by city planners) has declined as an avenue to status and has been largely usurped by the corporations.[8] Architectural historians of the future will have to write chapters on clients like Socony, Inland Steel, Crown-Zellerbach, and Manufacturers Trust.

The leisure of the old urban villager was meaningful chiefly as a release from work as a physical break. The leisure of the new suburban villager has increasingly become a status-conferring device. For some contemporaries, the functional uses of leisure, as in business golf, have completely obliterated the old distinctions between leisure and work. For a few, leisure means a search for the ancient meanings of recreation in some forms of self-fulfillment. This last-mentioned constructive leisure, however, is denied all but a few intellectuals in our society. We have invented no goals which would make such an activity truly meaningful for most people.

If the city of today is liberated from the old use of the surplus which created it, the citizens of the United States city find themselves buried under the burden of finding meaningful consumption. J. K. Galbraith, who was an ardent Keynesian in a time when employment and production were faltering in America, has since found the stimulation of employment and output a counsel of aimlessness in an affluent America.[9] To salvage meaning for his economic policy, he proposes using government spending to jack up lagging collective consumption and to redress the balance between "private opulence and public squalor." Private satisfaction from public achievement is little developed in the United States. Perhaps city planning can confer this kind of satisfaction. The task implies vast consumer education as well as proportionate ingenuity and creativity.

THE LEVELING OF URBAN CULTURE

In an environment in which work is meaningless and consumption needs to be constantly refurnished with gimmicks to be acceptable, the rate of the absorption of novelty is terrifying. Television has virtually given up trying for new plots, and has settled down with Westerns, a form of morality tale in which plot is unimportant. The tourism of Americans with money is reaching staggering proportions, expressed in dizzying itineraries in which new places are gobbled up at the rate of one or more a day. We are destined to exhaust our supply of "quaint" places as the speed and availability of transport makes "neighbors" out of the "foreigners."

Perhaps when the visible differences between places have disappeared (in Burchard's words, when the world is "one great Conrad Hilton chain") more subtle distinctions will be cultivated by the natives of the various cities in order to set the home town apart. But it is also possible that man's identification with a particular place will be weakened. Allegiance to a city or state is even now weaker for many than allegiance to a corporation, a profession, or a voluntary association. National allegiances survive because they have stronger functional implications—political system, economy, money, language, arms, etc. As long as one watches his clues to class and style, he can move from one American city to another with virtually no change in environment, as W. H. Whyte, Jr., has demonstrated.[10]

The second law of urban dynamics, were it written, would postulate that urban variety is running down fast. (Even now old-timers can acquire a semblance of distinction by picturing the "Old Tokyo" or "Old Bombay" before their Westernization.) The leveling has been most marked, not in the matters of subway systems, sewers, and skyscrapers, but in the whiskey-drinking habits of rising young French businessmen and the Coca-Cola breaks of the shop girls; it shows in the "beat" coffee shops of Japan and the omnipresent rock 'n' roll of teen-agers everywhere—an ironic comment on the slow progress of jazz up the Mississippi from New Orleans to Chicago in World War I America. Clearly, we have entered on an information-organization drive for the whole world that dwarfs the old task of taking the message to the small towns. Cities play a convenient role in this process, as the metropolis continues to provide a favorable habitat for a large volume of interchanges of information, but they are no longer essential to the task.

THE AUTONOMOUS GROWTH OF ORGANIZATION

Social as well as physical systems usually start out smaller than optimum size, and so can improve their efficiency by growth for a time. Efficiencies of various kinds provide the main impetus for organizations to "grow big." After a certain scale is reached, however, the original functions of the organi-zation may change. For at the "optimum scale" either a decline in efficiency sets in, or new tasks, appropriate to even greater size, are found.[11] The bigness in city forms, which is manifest in expressways and skyscrapers, housing projects and super-schools, supermarkets and chain stores, is paralleled by bigger metropolitan systems formed by the inclusion of more and more urban units. Within these systems, the individual units have changed many of their functions.

The extension of metropolitan organization to the relatively unorganized environs has been accompanied by restructuring and greater specialization. Settlements caught up in the wake have changed from market or retail centers to dormitories; local transport and utility systems have either been integrated into metropolitan systems or have disappeared in many in-stances. Most important, the small places have lost much of their sense of self-determination.

New York is the locale of an increasingly large proportion of the nation's economic decisions. Its relative importance as a setting for economic decision is enhanced by two important trends in the growth of economic organization: (1) the consolidations, mergers, and combinations which are grouping many "local" companies in single national organizations,[12] and (2) the extension of the market of regional producers to a national scale, facilitated by the improvement of interregional communication and transport and by the homogenization of regional tastes.

The corporation, which dominates American economic life, is not bound by local restraints. It moves freely across city and state lines. To grow bigger, it must extend its markets. When it extends them geographically, the dependence on any one place becomes relatively weaker.

THE DECLINING SOCIAL IMPORTANCE OF PLACE

To Plato, Aristotle, and Augustine, the "city" was a synonym for the ruling political and social organization of human relations and for the governing of man. In contemporary America, the corporation has largely usurped that image. Scott Buchanan has suggested that the corporation is the archetype of organization itself in our society, and its rules are the guide for the evolving form of our political relations.[13] To the extent that this is so, the concept of place, around which utopian reformers have woven the tapestry of the good life, will lose some of its meaning.

Corporations form larger organizations out of the amalgamation of smaller ones. Within the larger unit there is, after each addition, a careful preservation of the unity of direction. Decisions formerly made in Chicago or Boston must now emanate from New York.[14] Disappearing, together with some of the local-market direction of the society, is its counterpart, the local town-meeting democracy. Each now exists in isolated fringes only. Modified versions of local representation may well disappear as the cities themselves lose their old reasons for being. If cities become so specialized in function that citizens are members of the polity only on a part-time basis, while they are making economic decisions, working on a productive process, attending a conference, or vacationing (each in a different city), the old geographical basis for representation will have had the *coup de grâce*. For the wealthiest, most powerful, or most privileged of our society, this is already the case; their influence is exerted through "corporate," not geographical, channels, and it tends to gain primacy thereby.

Margaret Mead's picture of a future studded with highly specialized functional places, and a population traveling, as the occasion and interest demanded, from place to place among them for special-purpose conferences,[15] might well be the outcome of the high degree of wealth and transportation which made this movement possible, and of a social and political organization of our society which stripped the local places of any other reason for existence. Men, who came into the city to live only after a period of enjoying it from the relative freedom of afar, might now return to the wilds without giving up the city. What then would be the hold of any particular city?

THE CONSTRUCTIVE CITY

The cosmopolitan skimming of many cities is reserved for the world of affairs and power, for intellectuals and executives. The world of most others is still tied more closely to a single city. The marginal people in our society need the city and its supports, and they cannot afford isolation. For them community has come to mean the city. The aged, the handicapped, and the twenty to thirty per cent of our youth who will never get higher education in our time need to be in the mainstream of our society, not isolated from it. Idleness is an affront to their capacities and a barrier to self-esteem. Working mothers who need assistance in child care, minority groups, and deviants of all kinds seek tolerance, understanding, and assistance in the city. Our era's rejection of the city is also a symptom of its rejection of the productively underprivileged. The exurban drift of the more able is the fruit of a philosophy of individual survival.

Wherever industrial societies have not rejected the city, or have not used it badly, they have quarantined it. There is a present tendency for societies to turn the old city sections into living museums, as in the old walled center of Krakow.

The real challenge of the constructive city runs deeper than the preservation of medieval town centers girdled by green belts. It lies in the reconstruction of some of the sense of community which previously characterized the town and which inspires a good deal of the nostalgia with which the town is still regarded by some. It is too late to get this community back by any return to the soil or to handicrafts, or by some combination of these earlier technologies, in the manner suggested by Arthur Morgan or Ralph Borsodi or the Hassidic collectives of Israel.

Nor is it very constructive to propose a city in which communities are confined by social walls, with bazaar-like meeting places. The ghetto and the bazaar belong to an earlier society. Urbanization and industrialization have destroyed the old communal and feudal structures of social organization. As they come to maturity, they produce mass societies, pluralistic societies, or totalitarian societies, according to Kornhauser. To the extent that United States society is both pluralistic and organized into collateral systems, the old simple unity of communal life is gone. The community of place is also gone. Even the old pluralistic community of the marketplace has been broken down and replaced by the organization of corporate planning. We reject the corporate state of the totalitarian examples, but we have nothing to put in its place except empty statements about national purpose. National purpose can be immediate rather than remote; it can be addressed to the reconstruction of the world in which most Americans now live —the world of the metropolitan area. The strength of our productive power has prevented neither alienation nor impoverishment of opportunity. The logical heirs-apparent of the task of constructing cities to meet this challenge are the city planners. By tradition and temperament they are dreamers in the grand manner.

But the American city-planning movement has spent so much of its still young history trying to "get its feet on the ground" of local government that it is painfully space-bound. It is tied to the use of land and finds it difficult to rise to legitimate flights of fancy. It is hard pressed to utilize the findings of the army of analysts who have come into the movement to provide it with batteries of forecasts. Meier observes, "Often the study of a single innovation by itself, carrying through all the projections that are associated with it, leads to the conclusion that it should have a trivial impact and that the decisions concerning it should be relatively unimportant. However, it is not uncommon that two or three streams of small-scale innovation converge and a transition with major consequences results."[16]

As an aid to the necessary anticipatory thinking, Meier suggests the use of the fictional constructs employed by H. G. Wells and Edward Bellamy and by many lesser science-fiction writers. If they are to play the wholly warranted utopian role which has been left them by default, the city planners would do well to take up this challenge. Without attempting so ambitious an undertaking here, I would like to list a few of the concerns which might be treated in an imaginative picture of the constructive city of the future.

THE EDUCATIVE CITY

The leitmotiv that might be played throughout the picture is "The City as a Place of Learning." It seems that learning has always been the most powerful lure of the city; the city as a work place was expected to inculcate skills, and the city as a play place was expected to provide vices that were at least slightly instructive. The city as a show place was a place to wander about in, and gape at, and be shown.

The educative uses of the city have always been too numerous to be comprised in the curricula of the schools, but organized education has shown a marked affinity for the urban setting. In its medieval beginnings, the university was a creature of the city. The schools themselves cannot be ignored in the planning of the city. In addition, however, a wide variation in institutional auspices, ranging from the university through adult education and extension to the museums, libraries, and public places of the city, will house the total educational experience of the citizens. The public itself extends over many of these phases, and our concept of the "common education" can be extended to more of them.

A few years ago a group of architects and educators got together to work out a picture of the school of the future.[17] Their solution was a system in which the school was brought into the city, and the latter was turned into a total campus. This idea received the share of attention given to most novel school proposals, and then receded at the usual rate. It is unlikely that most educators interpreted it as anything more than a scheme for a wider use of field trips, for the proponents left enough conventional props of the school lying around to encourage this notion. But interpreted in more dynamic fashion, the scheme provides a beginning for an exploration of the potential dissolution of the barriers between school and city.

A more radical version of the educators' proposal would undertake the conscious design of the metropolis as an educational experience, rather than on the adaptive use of it. The aim would be to turn the city into an educational construct, with a view to providing a constant presence of meaning and a democratized form of learning.

The city that is devoted to the extension of opportunity would necessarily be an educative city. In the past, the extension of education, particularly to adults, has been aimed at facilitating social assimilation and upward mobility, and at remedying occupational deficiencies. For the genuinely underprivileged, our environment should continually be organized to these ends. But alienation is more widespread, reaching even into the economically more able. Here, education for noneconomic compensation must be extended. For these, it is not the education of the school, but the education of life experience which is most important. No sages can be found who can wisely prescribe the content of such experience, the best we can hope to do is to organize the opportunities for variety.

We live in an era in which formal schooling has largely supplanted apprenticeship, and the demands of skilled jobs have shifted from an emphasis on artistry to an emphasis on scientific literacy and communication skills so standardized that they can best be taught in school. The early contact with the world of real work cannot be re-established by occasional field trips. For the many who, for reasons of poverty of experience or other handicaps, cannot bridge the great gap between the arid abstractions of school and the conquest of the world of materials and men, schools that are truly "open" to the world and do not shut it out must be devised. If there are not apprenticeships left in industry, law schools, and architects' offices, there is still room for firsthand learning in citizenship, social relations, mass culture, and the management of one's affairs. The great advantage of cities at "human scale," or organized in comprehensible communities, is that an overview of the range of activities of a society is accessible.[18]

The problem, of course, would be more than an exercise in physical design, it would be a challenge to administrative ingenuity and social imagination. It would not do just to provide art and artifacts in ingenious arrangements. Means must be found for dislodging the presently frozen constellations of the urban ecology. For example, access to the educational experience of the *whole* city would have to be provided for all. In today's city, only a small part of the population experiences the whole city; slum dwellers are notoriously rooted to the corners and blocks of the small ethnic slum world, while the cosmopolitan professional middle class ranges the entire city. Free public transit would be an essential minimum step in the educational city. (The partial subsidy of the subway system by New York City makes Manhattan possible; the potential for an extension of this relation is untapped.)

Freedom to experience the city and learn its lessons is more than a matter of transit fares. It is a question of real freedom of choice, of power and acceptability. The West Side Puerto Rican or the Harlem Negro knows that he does not have access to the full meaning of the city of New York. Both the physical space apprehended by the individual and the Lewinian "life space" would have to be expanded. We make much of the city as a center of communication, but the information in the messages is received by a few, while to the many the communication content is chiefly noise.

It will be argued that most inhabitants of the city lack the equipment to receive this information and that their isolation in "ghettos" is self-imposed, a protective device against the confusion, stresses, and possible breakdown from this communication bombardment. There is no evidence, however, that the ordinary urbanite is at the limit of his information-handling capacity. Extension of this capacity is itself a major utopian goal in the constructive city.

Whatever is done, the city will be an instructional milieu. Anyone doubting this should reflect that it is the educative force of the city that many of our families now flee, for it is in the city that plural or strange values are taught their children. Families who would guard the education of their children fear this influence. Only when interclass and interethnic differences in value have been reduced somewhat will communication flow more freely.

THE OPEN CITY

Even the communication specialists will at times find the information interchanges of the city a strain. They will seek escape to relative privacy. Traditionally, it was available in the city, but even the golf course is a major center for information and decision in America. Abercrombie's plan for London sought to accommodate to this condition by providing a pre-cinctal organization of the city along functional and occupa-tional lines. In typical English fashion, these precincts were to offer some of the sociability of the club with a protected, inward-turning privacy, while permitting business to be car-ried on as usual.

It would be more typically American, however, to provide a truly open city. The open city would not be in the political grip of local cliques. It would be the antithesis of the old-time, one-industry, company town. In fact, in an era of truly cheap transport there is no need for conventional kinds of produc-tion to be in the city, and there is no need for people to live full time near their work. The open city belongs to the citizens who participate in its works.

There are many ways in which citizens can participate in experiments in the working of the city if the city is willing to experiment freely. For example, citizens can experience almost any day what it means to overload a highway system; the same lessons can be extended to other workings of the physical city and to its very government. "Tryout" stations can be set up for various kinds of urban apparatus, from conveyor sidewalks to expandable houses. The city government can rotate certain civic duties, like dining-room assignments at a boys' camp. It has been seriously suggested recently that citizens be depu-tized freely for the control of traffic violations. Such an action would be in the tradition of the colonial fire guards and citizen patrols who guarded the city at night. The losses in efficiency from the employment of less than optimum resources would not be crucial in an economy in which these resources were superabundant. It is important, however, that the civic duties in question be more than merely honorific; they must be func-tional in tangible respects.

Neither is there any need for the city to be the man's world while the suburbs belong to women, as is the case in America today. Only a relatively small part of the time charged to production in the city actually goes for that purpose. Much of the rest goes to a way of life, to the "business game." There is no need, other than the psychic requirements of the players, for maintaining this trend. Given greater choice, women might increasingly reject the exclusive role of consumer-specialist. As a society gets more remote from want, consumption as a class of activity loses importance and prestige. There are also signs that women of the leadership group, upper-middle-class style, are tending to a greater participation in politics. Business and politics, the great games of the city, should be opened to all its citizens.

The home—distant in psychological space and ground space but not in time from the city—would take less of a woman's day. Social planners have been slow to react to the steadily diminishing proportions of the average woman's life that are devoted to child-bearing and infant care.[19] Housewives frequently complain that the advent of a new household technology has actually lengthened their workday, but some of the additional work is managerial, and some is self-imposed to fill the void left by labor-saving devices. Given a chance to play more meaningful managerial roles, women would be able to divert sizable amounts of household time to the affairs of the city.

The open city is not, by contemporary standards, an efficient city. For a considerable time it would be a difficult and costly place to get things done. Such an open city could come about only as the result of the conscious choice of placing participation above product. Our town-meeting tradition even now does not work in big cities; but it continues to hold a place in our atavistic longings, and might be even more attractive if it could be rescued from the parochialism of suburbia or the dullness of the small town.

The productive technology, which grew in an intimate interdependence with the overhead economies of urbanization, has outstripped these facilitating arrangements and has become independent of them. The urban style of life of a growing proportion of the population has fed the demand for services, private and public. The old forms of the city are no longer needed, but the services the city provides are more than ever in demand. As these demands grow, it is necessary to devise means for "taking in each other's washing." One way to do this is to make rewarding leisure out of community service.

Unfortunately, the ingrained American respect for work and productivity not only prevents us from developing a genuine culture of community leisure but also robs us of respect for activities whose productive consequences are not apparent. This outlook, which is manifest in our treatment of the aged, the infirm, and the intellectually underprivileged, inhibits the full use of national energies and prevents those who cannot master the socially approved developmental tasks from experiencing full adulthood. As we face the prospect of an increasing difficulty in placing new entrants in the labor force,[20] it behooves us to consider some alternatives to the empty extension of education. Instead of brushing the youth out of sight in rural C.C.C. camps, let us consider placing them in the service of the city.

CONCLUSION

The exciting new cities of our time have virtually nothing to do with the old economies of city founding. Brasilia is as much a temple city, remote from the habitat and business of its people, as ancient Edith Shar. Chandigarh is as unessential to the economy of India as Mohenjo Daro. If cities can be built today as monumental symbols of national aspiration in countries poor by our standards, it is not so implausible to consider that we might build cities for our present needs and desired uses. At times cities are turned to vital uses in spite of the intentions of their builders, like the California town which started out to ape Venice and wound up, against its will, as a playground for motorcyclists.

The American construction industry is the world's most efficient, but the imaginative use we have found for it is the building of longer and better autobahns than were built by Hitler. We are unable to renew cities, not for lack of land planning but for lack of economic planning, and, more broadly, social policy. Looking at our metropolitan life, we find a deepened stratification, in social communication even more than in social ecology; a city in which management is in the hands of a meritocracy[21] recruited from the top fifteen per cent of the youth (the percent of high school students who now elect the academic major), a city in which a sizable part of the work force is in actual or disguised idleness but in which there are virtually no skills or traditions for making this idleness personally meaningful: a city in which there is a glut of goods and a paucity of public services.

Democracy cannot function where most of the demos is not needed, save as customer or ward. Yet democratic participation may actually get in the way of the functioning of our present cities, as C. Northcote Parkinson has suggested.[22] The answer need not be that of chucking local democracy; it may well be that of recasting our cities. But it is naïve to think that local democracy need be organized around the old notions of place-belonging, just as it is an oversimplification to believe that a physical relocation of the population will solve the functional problems of democracy in our industrial world.

Social invention and innovation in design need to converge on this task. The life style itself would be changed. Traditionally, these patterns are obdurate; but one may easily over-estimate the resistance of Americans to a change in life style. Spicer has noted the existence of a marked bias toward imputing such resistance to others on the part of those who are engaged in trying to bring about change or who are especially conscious of cultural differences.[23] People do resist change when it threatens their security; the change in the physical arrangements of city life would have to bulwark security rather than menace it. People tend to resist changes whose implications and workings they do not understand; the "new" forms must have elements of an earlier style (as the suburbs are related to rural small towns) which preserves some continuity. People may resist change if it is too abruptly and forcibly imposed; this is the hardest part of the process, for it requires involvement in change on the part of people who may lack the equipment desired, and so it means a willingness to pay high frictional costs.

Utopian thinking has a place in this process, not only in painting the consequences of failing to alter the present course, as Young recently, and Orwell, Huxley, and Ignatius Donnelley much earlier, have done, but also in sketching the possibilities of what might be, as Bellamy tried to do. Clearly, here is meaningful work enough for generations of American urbanists, if they can find in it the reward that will sustain them.

REFERENCES

1. The expected transition to a neotechnic complex, earlier formulated by Kropotkin and by Geddes, was applied by Mumford in *Technics and Civilization* (New York: Harcourt Brace, 1934), and *The Culture of Cities* (Harcourt Brace, 1938).

2. It is worth noting that the forecaster who was guided by considerations of engineering efficiency would never have acknowledged the potential since realized by the gas-driven auto. Only by blending in liberal amounts of judgment on income levels, social and individual motivation could he have come to an accurate forecast.

3. As a recent handbook points out, "Solar energy arrives in the neighborhood of the Earth at the rate of about 1.35 kilowatts per square meter." The capture of this energy for heat and power is the task of a new technology. Direct conversion of this energy into electricity via solar batteries, or into heat through some intermediate fluid or salt, makes possible an "emancipated" unit in which the power plant and the consumer are one. With adjustments in the collectors and the use of some standby conventional sources, this energy is available virtually everywhere.

4. Edward S. Deevey, "The Hare and the Haruspex," *The Yale Review*, Winter 1960, pp. 161-179.

5. *Ibid.*

6. Kingsley Davis in a recent paper for a seminar on urbanization in India at the University of California, Berkeley (June, 1960), painted the possibility of cities in India reaching a size of 60 million within the range of present forecasts.

7. Most recently, Paul Goodman, Harvey Swados, and others have updated this Veblenian theme. See Goodman's article, "Youth and Organized Society," *Commentary*, February 1960.

8. David Riesman, "New Standards for Old," reprinted in *Individualism Reconsidered* (Chicago: The Free Press, 1954), p. 228.

9. J. K. Galbraith, *The Affluent Society* (Boston: Houghton Mifflin, 1958).

10. W. H. Whyte, Jr., *The Organization Man* (New York: Simon and Shuster, 1956).

11. The less flexible species in history often perished from gigantism, particularly as their size reached the point where it generated demands the environment could not meet. As H. G.

Wells remarked, "In the record of the rocks it is always the gigantic individuals who appear at the end of each chapter." *Mind at the End of Its Tether* (New York: Didier Publishers, 1946), p. 25.

12. "Between 1949 and 1954, the number of mergers tripled. In recent years, two-thirds of all mergers have been of small companies into larger ones with assets of over $10 million." David T. Bazelon, "Facts and Fictions of U.S. Capitalism," *The Reporter*, September 17, 1959, p. 47.

13. Scott Buchanan, *The Corporation and the Republic* (New York: Fund for the Republic, 1959).

14. The firm for which my grandfather worked, which by virtue of its product, building materials, was both locally oriented and politically committed, is a good case. Whereas once it could not afford to be far from the meeting places of Chicago politicians, it has since grown big enough to acquire a different orientation, and recently merged with a firm operating largely in the field of defense contracts requiring it to be close to Washington decision-makers. The head offices of the combine will undoubtedly be in New York, where the nucleus of national decision-making is found.

15. Margaret Mead, "Values for Urban Living," *The Annals*, November 1957, pp. 10-14.

16. R. L. Meier, "Analysis of the Social Consequences of Scientific Discovery," *The American Journal of Physics*, 1957, 25: 611.

17. "Random Falls," feature article in *The School Executive*, March 1956.

18. The important point in this overview is not a mystical one of any special *Gestalt*, but resides in the power to choose more confidently when the alternatives are comprehensible.

19. Writing of British experience, Titmuss observed that at the beginning of the century, when the life expectation of a woman aged twenty was forty-six years, about one-third of this life expectancy would be destined for these activities. In 1956, however, when the life expectancy of a woman aged twenty was fifty-five years, only about 7 per cent of this life would be concerned with child-bearing and maternal care. R. Titmuss, *Essays on the Welfare State* (London: G. Allen & Unwin, 1958), p. 91.

20. In recent months (as of June, 1960) there has been some evidence that the seasonal peak in unemployment beginning with the end of the school term has been sharper than usual, and in some areas more than half the unemployed labor force is under

24 years of age. Within the next few years, employment prospects for new graduates are expected to become increasingly gray.

21. Michael Young, in his *The Rise of the Meritocracy, 1870-2033* (London: Thames and Hudson, 1958), has sketched the consequences of such a tendency in Britain in a social-fiction exercise much like that proposed here.

22. C. Northcote Parkinson, in an address at a national conference of the American Institute of Architects, San Francisco, April 21, 1960.

23. E. H. Spicer, Introduction to *Human Problems in Technological Change* (New York: Russell Sage Foundation, 1952), pp. 18-19.

9. Metropolitan Policy for Developing Areas

LLOYD RODWIN

THE POORER COUNTRIES of the world, that is, roughly speaking, those with an average per-capita income below $500, have most of the metropolitan problems of the wealthier countries plus a few unique to their circumstances, and they are subject to many more constraints. Their large cities also suffer from traffic problems. They have slums, blighted areas, and minority ghettos. Their open space is inadequate and badly distributed; and they, too, have miles of dull, grim, or ugly buildings. In addition, many of their cities endure illegal construction, the invasion of public land by squatters, and inadequacies in power, water supply, and drainage; and their metropolitan growth, accompanied by frenzied speculation in land, is concentrated in one or a few cities while development elsewhere is stunted.

Even such success in attacking the problems of economic development as these countries may achieve exacerbates some of their other problems, at least at the outset: rising incomes and improved prospects usually lead to more and larger families, a rising tide of migration, mounting traffic struggling through outmoded street systems, acute housing shortages, and crowding of houses and land. Inescapably, prices soar as a result of this pressure of an expanding demand for space and facilities on a supply that is relatively inelastic and inadequate. Add meager resources and a paucity of skilled professionals, and the immediate prospects are hardly encouraging. One thing is certain: the welter of problems cannot be decisively attacked piecemeal—that would be a labor of Sisyphus. If significant results are to be achieved within the next two or three generations, a radical strategy is essential.[1]

METROPOLITAN GROWTH: IS IT CONTROLLABLE?

The fact that growth does not take place the way we think it should is the essential common denominator of the metropolitan problems mentioned above. These problems underline the failure to anticipate economic and population expansion, or the lack of adequate mechanisms either to control, organize, or encourage desired patterns. However, it is not simply growth, but the location of growth that often fixes the scale, even the character, of these problems. If we could foresee where metropolitan expansion will occur, or if we could direct it to one place or another, we would have powerful weapons, and instead of our being overwhelmed, we might find that a few reasonably well-trained professionals could make an effective attack on these problems.

For example, wherever a flood of migrants from rural areas was anticipated, plans could be made to accommodate them. The arrangements (as in Puerto Rico) might cover only the minimum essentials, such as providing a small amount of land and a central source of water, together with instructions showing an individual how to build the simplest kind of dwelling with local materials. Even these modest efforts could result in a vast improvement over the unsanitary shanty towns now crowding the hills, the tidelands, the wastelands, and many of the public areas of almost every metropolis in developing countries. After a reasonable period, these efforts might also allow a stern policy, now virtually impossible, toward illegal mushroom settlements and violations of prescribed standards.

Moreover, some families and some activities could be steered to areas where development is desirable and away from those where further growth would inflame problems. Such control, like a thermostatic device, could alter the direction and scale of the flow at specified thresholds. In many developing countries, officials sometimes boggle at the expansion of the capital (or largest metropolis) at a rate greater than appears justified by the growth of economic activities, while little or no development prevails in other regions. Some migration away from the land might be channeled to other foci of economic and social opportunity. Such cities as Caracas, Istanbul, Djakarta, and Mexico City exhibit a disproportionately huge consumption of scarce resources for expensive community overhead investments (ports, roads, water supply, power installations, housing, etc.)—a situation hardly justifiable either in terms of the goals of national development or the possible long-run returns from concentrated investments in other regions.

If power were exercised to regulate metropolitan growth, it would provoke debate and investigation on the nature of such growth. One could expect controversy on whether there are optimum distributions of cities of different size,[2] and what effects different patterns of urban development would have on costs, productivity, the birth rate, military security, and a variety of other considerations. Perhaps this is as it should be. It has too long been taken for granted that the scale and character of the metropolis must be the end product of a multitude of separate decisions of firms and families—subject, some might add, to the proviso that whatever problems arise might be corrected later in the fullness of time. In theory, however, urban scale and pattern could be projected for the nation as a whole, and the economy and the social system directed to adjust accordingly. Or, less cavalierly, an effort could be made to steer toward some preferred pattern, taking into account trends, costs, feasibility, and other relevant factors.

THE CASE FOR CONCENTRATED DECENTRALIZATION

Strictly speaking, this hypothetical ability to anticipate or influence growth presupposes no particular philosophy or ideal of development. To the extent this is feasible, this power could be used to promote either one huge center, a few major centers, a network of decentralized communities, or some combination of these. The decision makers in each country would be obliged only to recognize that urban patterns could be treated as variables subject to modification to serve various purposes. They would have to decide far more explicitly than now which policy would best suit their problems, their values, and their goals of development. Most countries, however, would find the policy of encouraging metropolitan concentration in a few regions a desirable one for several reasons. To begin with, the meager resources make it impossible to pursue a systematic policy of dispersion. Since there are not enough resources for all communities and regions, some principle of selection is unavoidable. The encouragement of smaller cities is one possibility, and it has some advantages. From 50 to 70 per cent, approximately, of the total capital available for investment goes into community "overhead."[3] Many of these costs are probably higher in the larger cities. Moreover, with most of the facilities of these cities overtaxed, the marginal costs of accommodating a much larger population are likely to be high. The proponents of decentralization believe:[4]

Cheap land, lower densities and shorter distances could mean simpler standards and technology for all kinds of social and civic facilities, utilizing rough, impermanent materials, personal labor and capital otherwise untapped, and other resources from the more or less non-monetized sectors of the economy. From this viewpoint, decentralization in one form or another is essentially a resource-saving device.

On the other hand, it is more important to increase returns than to cut costs. Through processes not as yet fully understood, growth appears to have a better chance of becoming self-propelling in the larger cities, that is, cities of 100,000 or more. This is likely to be especially true of those with some initial advantages, such as an exceptional harbor, a salubrious climate, superior transport, preferably with access to a potentially rich hinterland, or a resource ripe for exploitation. Such assets offer a matrix of opportunities which, if successfully exploited, will create new advantages and opportunities: a larger and more specialized labor force, more adequate credit and exchange facilities, increased business and professional services, improved roads and utilities, more diversified job opportunities, a wider range of consumer services sparking worldly ambitions and competitive effort. The interaction of such developments creates external economies, widens the market, generates new enterprises—in short, reinforces the whole syndrome of growth and radiates its influence over an expanding hinterland.

Large cities also attract migrants and induce drastic changes in traditional attitudes. Job opportunities or illusions beckon; and so do the jostling crowds, the bazaar-like shops, and the rich variety of sights, sounds, and human experience. Patterns of family expenditures change, standards of demand rise, the birth rate tends to decline, the origins of class or caste lose some of their significance, while innovations find an easier welcome. Such influences do not happen overnight, of course. No one knows how many derive from increased income and education, new patterns of work and living, or to what extent the scale of the metropolis itself plays a role—and if the latter, which urban size, or mixture of sizes, produces the best results. During the next decade research may give us a lead on these matters.[5] For the moment we have only a strong suspicion, supported by what we observe of urban trends in economically advanced countries, that a shift from the traditional peasant economy to that of the large city is conducive to these results, and that, given the objective of encouraging economic progress, we may regard these as the desirable aspects of urbanization.

However, partly because of the probable advantages of large cities, the present trend in most of these countries is leading to a politically unacceptable and potentially explosive dualism:[6]

A peasant agriculture and handicrafts sector using simple labor intensive techniques where manhour productivity is extremely low, and where one-half to four-fifths of the population earn their incomes; and a plantation-mining-and-manufacturing sector using advanced techniques where manhour productivity is high but where only a small part of the population is employed. . . . Both sectors are usually distinct geographically as well as technologically and economically. Sometimes they represent quite different regions. Nearly always the two sectors appear in a contrast between one or a few large and growing cities and the surrounding countryside— Djakarta, Surabaya and Indonesia; Delhi, Bombay, Calcutta and India; Manila and the Philippines; San Juan and Puerto Rico; Harcourt and Nigeria; Tripoli and Libya—the examples can be extended to virtually every underdeveloped country.

This dualism is probably responsible for an inefficient allocation of capital. The losses are hard to estimate but are nonetheless real: they involve not so much the increasing costs for overhead, transportation, and congestion in the one or two expanding cities as the costs (even harder to calculate) resulting from the failure to exploit resources and other investment possibilities in the lagging regions. In the largest cities opportunities come more easily within the line of vision of the investors, whereas in other areas the lack of information makes it difficult to judge whether opportunities there might not be more remunerative. Even when information becomes available the prospects are still apt to be obscure. Returns must be gauged over a long period, and during the first few years when prediction is somewhat surer, the returns may be low, though thereafter they may more than balance higher returns elsewhere. Success also tends to fan expectations, failure, to dampen them. Under these circumstances, Hirschman is quite justified in concluding that "the external economies [in growing areas], although real, are consistently overestimated by the economic operators."[7]

Perhaps the most effective means of correcting these estimates, aside from general policies on taxation and incentives, is through government decisions on the location of overhead facilities; but there are two powerful forces that lead to questionable allocations: the pressure to supply the overhead facilities required or induced in the growing metropolis; and the pressure (both for political reasons and the lack of adequate technical talent) to disperse resources earmarked for regions outside the large cities "among a large number of small projects scattered widely over the national territory."[8] The question that constantly faces responsible officials, therefore, is how to channel investments so that they will not be frittered away in dispersed efforts throughout the country or else expended in the big cities on costly urban services that could well be postponed. Ideally, the decision-makers should husband this capital so as to create opportunities for investment and thus stimulate selected growing points, or impulse sectors.

The policy most likely to achieve current goals would seem to be the creation of several regional centers (including essential transportation links, minimum overhead facilities, and the necessary intelligence mechanisms, so as to examine more systematically the possibilities for development). If such a policy were clearly defined, it would place private investors in a far better position to judge the prospects of the area; and it would also make it possible for government officials to evaluate plans for capital expenditure for railroads, highways, power installations, utilities, housing, and other community facilities, to be sure that they contributed whenever feasible to the success of these centers. The relative concentration would aid some of these regional centers to acquire some of the characteristics of what Perroux calls *poles de croissance*,[9] and thus to compete more effectively with the existing metropolis, and even help spark a profound transformation in the cultural pattern of the hinterland. The growth of such regional centers would also enable the capital cities to cope more effectively and economically with the population avalanche that now threatens them.

Of course, it will not be simple to break the vicious cycle and ensure that these investments in regional centers are not

made prematurely or unwisely. Much depends on the right
selection of such centers. Even so, individual firms may see no
advantage in shifting their location until the necessary overhead facilities exist. Moreover, the provision of such facilities
is "permissive," and may not always induce the desired entre-
preneurial activity.[10] Probably only one or two centers can be
developed in the early period of economic development, because there is only a rather limited national market, and
because much of the investment will be made in agriculture,
transport, and communications, thus involving considerable
geographical dispersion. As the economy expands, however,
regional markets emerge, and industry becomes more oriented
to labor and market. Larger urban centers are then more
feasible. Notwithstanding the difficulties, the promotion of
regional centers may have a better chance for acceptance than
a plan that neglects the lagging areas, and may well prove
more effective in promoting the various goals of development
than either dispersion or concentration in one or two great
cities would be.

POLICY IMPLICATIONS

There are some important corollaries to the realization of
such a program. First of all, there will be an administrative
need to formulate a national policy for metropolitan development. A lack of skilled professional staff would make it necessary for a few key specialists to work through some national
agency where the proper studies could be carried on. A few
other specialists would cover critical metropolitan regions to
help carry the program into effect. Such centralized effort
would not be foreign to the political tradition of most poor
countries, where the central government is usually strong and
the local authorities weak. Nevertheless, the creation of a national policy would be a novel exercise, especially for physical
(city and regional) planners.[11] By training and experience
their function has been to formulate goals, to determine prospects for growth and changes in requirements for the use of

land, and to devise policies and control mechanisms so that physical development should be consistent with the goals for the city and the region. To devise a national policy for metropolitan development they must deploy their skills for the physical development of the entire nation. Most planners today would have to learn this task in doing it, for educational programs have only recently begun to make appropriate adaptations to serve such a need.

Another corollary will be the obligation to relate economic (and, where appropriate, social) policies for the nation to those worked out for metropolitan development. Most developing countries now have some sort of economic policy or planning mechanism for promoting growth. Such agencies generally define the economic goals, evaluate the available resources and economic opportunities, and suggest appropriate policies—fiscal, monetary, budgetary, exchange, development, etc. For the most part the analyses are aggregative and are formulated in terms of trends and the requirements of output, employment, income, savings, investment, etc. On occasion there may be location tags attached to plans for specific capital investments such as roads, multipurpose valley programs, resettlement projects, harbor installations, and irrigation schemes. On the other hand, location analysis is usually slighted or at best discursively touched on, if considered at all. The reason is:[12]

Economic development plans concentrate on capital use. They do not as a rule include a plan for land use as such. Decisions as to land use are left to private investors, local governments and to central government implementing agencies within the framework of capital allocation which is provided in the economic development plan. Presumably, if an appropriate allocation of capital is obtained, the appropriate allocation of management, labor and land will follow substantially.

As a result of this convenient assumption, economists have generally neglected such questions as where growth should occur, on what scale, and over what period. Most economists

now working on plans for economic development have not
been specifically trained and have only a marginal interest in
the metropolitan or regional aspects of development. It is not
surprising, therefore, that analysis of local or regional economic prospects or of feasible alternatives for development, or
of the relations between the rural and urban sectors, has been
only negligible. This is true of almost all present plans for
developing areas such as India, Indonesia, the Philippines,
Turkey, or Mexico.

The gulf between physical and economic planning further
complicates matters. The low esteem in which local and regional studies are still held inhibits most top-rank graduates in
economics and the other social sciences from developing a
serious interest along these lines. Development economists also
function in a different sphere of government, use esoteric
language, utilize different methods of analysis, and in general
distrust "do-gooders," a class in which they often place city
and regional planners. In developing countries the instinctive
reaction of the economist to the city planner is to wonder
whether the economy can afford the luxury of "the city beau-
tiful," or whatever other frills he imagines the city planner is
contemplating. The latter, on the other hand, is not infre-
quently full of scorn for the economist for limiting himself to
convenient national aggregates and for misapplying textbook
principles, without any real understanding of the effects of his
decisions on urban and regional possibilities. Neither image
is flattering or just,. yet each continues to influence attitudes.

Nevertheless, there has recently been a remarkable growth
of interest in urban and regional studies. The upsurge promises
to produce social scientists interested in regional and interregional aspects of development and physical planners who
can understand the economists' models and who can formulate
some models of physical development of their own. It is precisely in this fitting together of independent models for development, both theoretically and in the field, that linkages
and joint efforts are needed and are likely to come.

For example, we need some reformulation of the goals of development. It will not do to think simply in terms of full employment, levels of output, optimum rates of growth, maximum net social product, etc. There may be a variety of metropolitan alternatives consistent with any agreed-on set of economic targets; and it is possible that some metropolitan patterns are more likely than others to achieve these objectives. It only begs the question to assume that the proper patterns will sort themselves out automatically. Whether they will in fact do so is precisely the question. Both the economists and the physical planners, therefore, will be obliged to examine the feasible alternatives and submit their recommendations to the appropriate decision-makers.

We shall also have to evaluate the potentials for developing metropolitan regions. At present the emphasis in economic policy has been "vertical," that is, on developing particular sectors of the economy such as transportation, power, agriculture, education, forestry, etc. This emphasis tends to neglect the symbiotic character of a region and the interdependence of its diverse activities.[13] The advantages of this vertical or sector approach would be greatly enhanced if there were a parallel "horizontal" evaluation of the most significant problems, prospects, and requirements for growth of the regions. We need models to indicate the present and feasible levels of economic activity, the projections of population, the available choices in goals, and specific recommendations for policy. The implications can then be traced for trends in migration, requirements for ports and roads, housing, shopping, education, health and cultural facilities. With such models, the officials would be better placed to evaluate the relative importance of capital expenditures and the proper time for making them, within an over-all policy for developing each region.

The effects of various national policies on metropolitan development must also receive some attention. We have already noted the influence of the location and priority schedules for overhead capital, such as rail and highway development.

Similarly, policies for tariffs, taxes, and amortization of plant, the location of government installations, the projects of agencies for economic development, official attitudes to village patterns of living, and urban migration are examples of other national activities that influence metropolitan development. Such influences, however, are generally the unintended consequences of efforts to do something else. If the goals for metropolitan development were clarified, the effects of some of these policies and programs could be examined and, when appropriate, adjusted so as better to achieve the declared objectives of the nation.

HYPOTHETICAL INSTITUTIONAL REQUIREMENTS

Can we be more specific about the hypothetical institutional requirements for a national policy on metropolitan development, and also the problems such a policy is likely to encounter in developing areas? The answer is yes. A first approximation is possible, provided we make certain assumptions as to the aims and functions of the central government. A national urban policy would presuppose: (a) a stable government that seeks to guide urban development in a manner consistent with economic progress and the social and political ideals of the country; (b) some central intelligence and control mechanisms by which it can be decided what influence the government should wield on physical and economic development; (c) some central power over the principal mechanisms for allocating capital, since, for a variety of reasons, the local governments and the private sector are relatively weak, as a rule; (d) a relatively efficient civil service. The economy, however, may be private, public, or mixed, and of course there would have to be certain modifications in detail, depending on the various political and cultural contexts.

Within such constraints, a metropolitan or regional development function could be included either in the chief executive's office, or in a national planning agency, or in some national agency for public works and metropolitan development. Its officials would be responsible for the formulation of a national policy coordinate with the policy for the development of the national economy. Their task would be to study economic and population trends, the potentials and limitations in resources, the functions, patterns, and possibilities for development of the country's urban and metropolitan communities, plans and prospects for industrial, agricultural, or village development, and plans for transportation and power networks. They would divide the country into development regions and evaluate the implications of alternative policies, including the difficulties of implementation; and they would submit a digest of the feasible policies and the reasons for their recommended course of action to the chief executive and other responsible officials.

Ideally, a rational planning system for the central and local government agencies would be essential. The principal departments of the government, particularly those concerned with development, would prepare plans. These would deal with present and prospective operations and targets. Similarly, local and regional plans for channeling development, private and public, would be necessary. Each agency would have to make its plans consistent with national policy. Some agencies would need considerable assistance in preparing and coordinating plans with other programs. Therefore, there must be one group responsible for technical assistance, coordination, and review. This group would have to familiarize itself with local and central government programs, provide advice, interpret the general policy, and coordinate related plans. Their staff would include area specialists acquainted with metropolitan and regional plans and with actual experience in specific localities. These specialists would serve a valuable feedback function by reporting to the central agency and the officials responsible for capital budgeting information about area plans and needs, the performance in the field, and problems that otherwise might be overlooked.

Regional capital budgets would also be advisable. Such

budgets would not be formulated as are data for national income or budget—that would be too difficult. Instead, the proposed budgets of all the departments of the central government could be transferred to a set of forms indicating the regional incidence of capital expenditures. By some device such as "development maps," it would be possible to see at a glance where capital expenditures have been undertaken in the past and where they are being planned. At first there might be some difficulty in obtaining the requisite data on a comparable basis, and it would be necessary to obtain the best first approximations. Then, over a period, it should be possible to develop forms on which the several ministries could supply information, using standard definitions of items classified as capital expenditure. These data would then be shifted to forms summarizing all capital expenditures within a region, and these in turn could be easily mapped.

Such maps would provide valuable and easily understandable information on the implicit development policy of the nation. They would also establish a basis for gauging programs, both proposed and under way, in any particular region, and whether complementary requirements were being taken into account. When metropolitan and regional plans become available, the development maps could also be compared with the development goals so as to measure progress.

PROBLEMS OF IMPLEMENTATION

It would be fashionable, and perhaps not even inaccurate, to characterize the above ideas as a policy model. Its purpose is to suggest how a national strategy on metropolitan development could be devised and adapted to the cultural, economic, and political goals and institutions of a hypothetical underdeveloped country. The proposals are either the equivalents or the rough extensions of mechanisms for economic policy now available in many of these countries. The effective shaping of urban policy is likely only when similar institutions exist for dealing with metropolitan issues on a national scale, especially in so far as they interact with the basic investment and development policies of the central government. Experts from various countries can best judge what legislation and institutional changes are necessary for our model, what social attitudes are implied, and what other factors may be relevant for applying the model to their respective countries.

Although the issues our scheme poses may vary, at least three problems will confront every country. First is the question of personnel, which is critical; specialists in these problems are rare, and, as we have observed, few have ever received the professional training for some of the responsibilities involved. Second is the level of intellectual capital. Whether we now know enough about these problems to discharge such responsibilities effectively is debatable. Many would doubt whether we can secure the necessary understanding early enough to avoid doing more harm than good. Third, the proposed innovations in policy may accentuate tendencies for political centralization. Many of these countries are already suffering from "apoplexy in the center and anemia at the edges." Sooner or later their governments will have to decentralize operations. It should be the task of the central government to call the signals and permit local or regional agencies to conduct more of the actual operations.

To cite these difficulties is likely to produce contrary reactions. Some will find decisive arguments against such a program, others will brush aside the problems or consider them problems to be solved. One of the dangers in developing countries is the desire to bite off more than can be chewed. Even the economically advanced countries, it will be said, would have difficulties in bringing such programs to a successful conclusion—witness the problems Great Britain had with the New Towns. There is enough in these arguments to cause responsible persons to hesitate and weigh the consequences. But the choice between all or nothing may not be necessary. Some of the hypothetical recommendations can stand alone. For some countries it may be enough simply to establish a high-level group concerned with the national policy for metropolitan or regional development. Officials in these countries may want to explore the ideas but may be unwilling to set up the more intricate planning system. Other countries may reap immediate dividends by undertaking thorough regional studies or by establishing a mechanism to budget and evaluate the regional incidence of capital expenditure. Still others might wish to go much farther, for surely the argument for more extensive action is not without appeal. Decisions are daily being made for fixing future patterns of development. These decisions are already creating grave problems for the future. Is it not better to make these decisions consciously? True, there are disheartening obstacles, but would not the same arguments in favor of inaction also apply to economic and foreign policies? And, if it is essential for a nation's growth and security to develop sophisticated economic policies, may not national policies on metropolitan development be likewise justified to support the objectives of economic, social, and physical development?

REFERENCES

1. This responsibility cannot be handled simply by the price system. The difficulties are already manifest in the widespread concern with urban maladjustments. We know the market for urban land and improvements is characterized by imperfect knowledge, sluggish or inflexible adjustments to price signals, and significant discrepancies between public and private costs. We know, too, that many of the basic decisions on urban development are not, and for some practical purposes cannot be, made by the market mechanism. They involve public policy on the kind of systems for controlling the use of land and decisions on the public investment of capital for urban overhead. In part these decisions are induced responses to private activity; but equally—perhaps even oftener—in these developing countries they must anticipate and shape the framework or the channels for public and private activity.

2. For example, see R. Vining, "A Description of Certain Spatial Aspects of an Economic System," *Economic Development and Cultural Change*, 1955, *3:* 147-195; also E. M. Hoover, "The Concept of a System of Cities: A Comment on R. Vining's Paper," *ibid.*, 196-198; and W. F. Stolper, "Spatial Order and the Economic Growth of Cities: A Comment on Eric Lampard's Paper," *ibid.*, 137-146.

3. Paul Rosenstein-Rodan supplied me with these figures as part of studies not yet published. The estimates are based on data for several countries, and of course the figures vary for each country. See also P. N. Rosenstein-Rodan, "Les Besoins des Capitaux dans les Pays Sous-Développés," *Economie Appliquée*, 1954, nos. 1-2, pp. 77-89.

4. Catherine Bauer Wurster, "The Nature and Cost of Minimum Acceptable Living Conditions in Different Types of Indian Urban Community" (mimeographed), Department of City and Regional Planning, University of California, Berkeley.

5. See E. E. Lampard, "The History of Cities in Economically Advanced Areas," *Economic Development and Cultural Change*, 1955, 3: 81-136; B. F. Hoselitz, "Generative and Parasitic Cities," *ibid.*, 278-294; B. Harris, "Urbanization Policy in India," *Papers and Proceedings of the Regional Science Association*, 1959, 5: 181-207. For a very different source of suggestive ideas,

see F. Perroux, "Note sur la Notion de 'Pole de Croissance,'" *Economie Appliquée*, 1955, 8: 307-320.

6. C. Haar, B. Higgins, and L. Rodwin, "Economic and Physical Planning: Coordination in Developing Areas," *Journal of the American Institute of Planners*, 1958, 24: 169.

7. A. O. Hirschman, *The Strategy of Economic Development* (New Haven: Yale University Press, 1958), pp. 184-185. Hirschman shrewdly goes on to explain, "The reason for this tendency— perhaps implicit in the phrase 'nothing succeeds like success' —must be sought in the realm of social psychology. The progressive sectors and regions of an underdeveloped economy are easily overimpressed with their own rate of development. At the same time, they set themselves apart from the less progressive operators by creating a picture of the latter as lazy, bungling, intriguing and generally hopeless. There seems to be a cliquishness about progress when it first appears that recalls the same phenomenon among adolescents. . . . Even though the initial success of these groups may often be due to sheer luck or to environmental factors such as resource endowment, matters will not be left there. Those who have been caught by progress will always maintain that they were the ones who did the catching; they will easily convince themselves or attempt to convince others that their accomplishments are primarily owed to their superior moral qualities and conduct. It is precisely this self-righteousness that will tend to produce its own evidence: once these groups have spread the word that their success was due to hard work and virtuous living, they must willy-nilly live up to their own story, or at the least will make their children do so. In other words, there is reason to think that the 'Protestant ethic,' instead of being the prime mover, is often implanted *ex post* as though to sanctify and consolidate whatever accumulation of economic power and wealth has been achieved. To the extent that this happens, a climate particularly favorable to further growth will actually come into existence in the sectors or regions that have pulled ahead, and this will confirm the economic operators in their preference for these regions and make it somewhat less rational" (pp. 185-186).

8. *Ibid.*, pp. 190-192. See also S. H. Robock, "Regional and National Economic Development in India," *Papers and Proceedings of the Regional Science Association*, Washington, D. C., December 1959.

9. F. Perroux, *loc. cit.*, reference 5.

10. Hirschman, *op. cit.*, pp. 190-197.

11. Throughout this paper the term "physical planners" is used as a synonym for city and regional planners.

12. C. Haar, B. Higgins, L. Rodwin, *op. cit.*, p. 168.

13. Often these allocations grow out of requests from provincial and state authorities, but they are rarely the result of careful studies of the economy and growth potentials of various regions or even an estimate of the complementary requirements resulting from proposals for development in these regions. In part, the absence of these evaluations and the crudeness of the aggregative decisions in many countries account for the constant record of complaint about disproportions to be found in the studies and reports on the progress of economic development: the discovery of agricultural development without marketing facilities; ports without feeder roads; power installations without market outlets; and industries without adequate shopping, housing, and community facilities. See P. G. Frank, "Economic Planners in Afghanistan," *Economic Development and Cultural Change*, 1953, *1:* 339; and the International Bank for Reconstruction and Development, *The Economic Development of Mexico* (Baltimore: The Johns Hopkins Press, 1953), pp. 150-151.

10. Notes on Expression and Communication in the Cityscape

GYORGY KEPES

OUR SOCIETY EXHIBITS, in addition to a small body of explicit symbols—the signs or tags, verbally or otherwise coded, orientationally or otherwise directed, with unequivocal messages delivered by visual means—a vast body of implicit symbols of all kinds. Just as the way in which we respond to our environment gives shape to our social structures and our arts, our social structures and our arts provide mute testimony of the quality of our responses to our environment. This is testimony that we can read—with all shades of clarity and depth of understanding, in proportion to our own aptness of response to the objects and events that we encounter.

At its simplest level, the *implicit symbol* that provides this mute testimony is almost indistinguishable from the explicit sign—for example, the initialed sweater that proclaims the officially accredited college athlete. Such sweaters and such initials, our society agrees, are the conventional indexes by which we are to recognize men who have distinguished themselves in physical sport. Similarly, the Phi Beta Kappa key proclaims socially recognized mental attainment.

There are other indexes that, if less official, are equally socially generated. Juvenile delinquents have their uniforms of horsehide jackets, belt buckle, blue jeans, and boots; beatniks are bearded; undergraduates wear crew cuts, soft-tailored tweed jackets, and slim trousers. We absorb these conventions as part of our acculturation. In a different context of visual meaning, trained archeologists, through the internal evidence of style in historically evolved forms, can determine within a decade or two the date of a piece of statuary or a carved bit of tracery. No matter how modern the guise, a church is recognized by everyone as a church, because of the persistence of familiar trends that go as far back as the era of Constantine. And we recognize a bank as a bank even more easily now than we did when banks wore the outer trappings of Greek temples; the inner array of counters, tables, giant vault door, and desk is still the same, although purified into more elemental shapes and colors, and the vast expanse of glass now permits us to see this inner structure directly from the sidewalk or the road.

Our immediate experiences trigger our memories, releasing the cognate images from our stored experience into the temporary focus of awareness and establishing a relation between our present and our past. This is obviously true of our personal, individual, uncommunicated experience, but it is also true of the stored-up experience that we share with other persons of our condition—our profession, our town, our income bracket, our political party, our religion, our nation, our century. Some images are common images, some symbols, common symbols. Without common symbols, men could not have evolved very far above the animal level; but with them men have gone in a mere five or six thousand years from simple to ever more complex social levels. The socialization, or standardization, of such spatial divisions as the length of the human foot or the thickness of the human thumb or the weight of a stone became unit spatial measurements, unit weight measurements, or unit monetary measurement according to the selected index, or symbolic connective characteristic, thus establishing the social basis of technology and science.

Foci of common life—the family home, the community church or school—command the individual and collective respect of the group involved. They symbolize common life as well as house it. In giving concrete shape to our awareness, such symbols give rise to expressive, manifestly significant forms, molding and creating our arts and rituals. Monumental —self-consciously impressive—architecture arose many thousands of years ago out of the need felt to call attention to the place where men met to deal with their important common problems. From Stonehenge to the Athenian Agora, from the Forum Romanum to the United Nations building, the place of assembly has formed and been formed by the power of impressive design. The forms have varied according to need and according to the different type of cooperative activity considered necessary to group survival. Over the centuries, of course, the radius of group involvement has increased. The different scales of a New England common and Rockefeller Plaza indicate changing concepts of human cooperation; but, whatever the range of interest that these urban forms may express, there can be no doubt that they perform a symbolic function. They are symbols of a common perceptual reality, and, as such, belong to a common symbolic world. Without the images of this world, the growth of the urban environment could not be guided or controlled.

JUXTAPOSITION OF SYMBOLS

In the visual field, particularly in the successive images that we perceive in our environment, the juxtaposition of images offers the most potent symbolic qualities. The contrast of the towering cathedral with the cluster of small dwellings in a medieval city had a symbolic quality. In some of the great cities of the Near East, the bleak, undifferentiated long span of the desert, offset by the flamboyant richness of the clustered buildings, created a perceptual tension with great symbol-evoking power. In our cities, the juxtaposition of very large with very small buildings, of busy with tranquil areas, are more than simple expressions of variety. Contemporary urban dwellers living in a restrained, almost inhuman setting usually welcome every sign of the natural world that can be introduced.

Central Park is more than a pleasant means for escaping the busyness of the city; in its juxtaposition with a surrounding frame of high buildings it is a symbol of the richness and strength of metropolitan existence. It is self-evident that the architect or planner cannot consciously create this grand scale of poetry with such symbolic juxtapositions; but, on the other hand, awareness of the power and meaning of contrasting forms is necessary if we are to guide the shaping of a rich poetic city. In the intricate and numerous visual-sequence relationships that the city offers its population, meanings are conveyed in accordance with the structure of the sequence path that we follow.

We read the personality of a man through observing the sequence of his expressions and actions. We read the character of the cityscape in the same way. A single-cell organism is immediately dependent on its environment, and has no means of controlling it. Only when cells grow into complex masses do they develop a fixed internal organization capable of protecting them from change or disturbance in the external environment. In this complex stage there is a division of labor, with the functioning of specific organs coordinated. In a complex social state, a similar structuring develops. Under primitive conditions, individuals are free to move. In the complex production processes of our civilization, the division of labor and the physical stability of the work place bring about a relative fixation of the individual in the group. His mobility is a highly limited one. From home to work, from work to home, from home to shopping, the individual follows a defined path at a specified time. Each path of travel offers its characteristic challenge. The basic unit of our urban vision, accordingly, is not the fixed spatial location but the transportation-defined pattern of a sequence of vistas.

Let us compare the succession of impressions from opposite directions in a sequence experience. A commuter usually takes the same route in entering and leaving the city, but the elements of the sequence experience are in reverse order. Entering, he sees calm, well-groomed suburbia; then the industrial outskirts; then the belt of slums; then the heavy traffic and kaleidoscopic variety of the business area. In the sequence each shift of vista conveys meaning. The jump from the tidy, pastoral quality of the suburban area to the garbage dumps and smoke rings of the industrial outskirts inevitably gives rise to some feeling in the perceptive traveler. Going home, he finds similarly that the sequence of scenes from the power-suggestive industrial plants to the inhuman substandard dwellings of the industrial slums is charged with larger meanings. The same form elements, in reverse order, evoke different responses. The succession of distances and the strength of the impacts are compositional elements of symbolic significance.

It is evident that without a major restructuring of the environment this chain of images cannot be modulated. But an analysis of their impacts can bring significant understanding and, possibly, tools for shaping and controlling parts of the environment. An awareness of the qualities of meaning evoked in the spectator by certain sequence relations of morphological elements would help him to develop the sensitivity necessary for forming sound judgments. There is a potential new keyboard of creative formation that can be understood with the aid of technical tools, such as motion pictures, and it may be used with increasing scope. A careful survey of the relationships of form elements in succession is the necessary beginning. Sequential relations of open and closed space, high and low buildings, rich or simple surfaces, natural features and man-created forms, and the many other variables, can be studied, recorded, and manipulated in order to gain some feeling for the expressive qualities inherent in the juxtaposed features in the sequence chain. Regular and irregular changes, rhythmical or contrapuntal sequences of different space distances, have to be recorded and interpreted. The range is too vast to be brought down to experimental testing, but there are means for helping us to understand these processes.

Because of the enlarged scale and increased complexity of the metropolitan environment, one central core as an expression of civic connectedness is insufficient for all purposes. There is an increasing need to express in symbolic form not one co-operative act, but the interrelatedness of the whole urban field. Architectural history suggests a procedure common to all cultures: the emphasizing of structurally important elements. To reveal the cooperative functions of the separate structural members, master builders and architects have accented the primary weight-carrying members, especially at the critical points of their function. There is a similar possibility in the broader scale of city structure. Dominant functional areas that reveal significant cooperative effort can also be articulated by decorative means appropriate to the scale and dimensions of the city. In our present cityscape the various areas are undefined. The basic characteristic of our present life is inter-dependence, but the molding expressive symbols of this interdependence are still missing.

The exploded space of the metropolis in which effective distance depends upon the mode of travel and in which vast areas and populations become linked in a single urban fabric makes the unit building or unit area a less important symbol than in the past. We must find contemporary substitutes and expressive symbols of these new dynamic dimensions. This is especially difficult when the parts of the city are unclear; often today, when one drives in from a suburban residential area to the working center of a city, the sequence of scenes is chaotic, its connecting links are lost, and its symbolic significance is still-born. What is actually expressed is chaotic, haphazard growth. But the city's parts can be made clear, and a restudy of the sequence of vistas in expressive continuities can offer new symbols. Sharp accents signifying character changes between two areas give legibility and underline the structural logic of the total urban scene. The heights of buildings, open or closed spaces, changing color schemes, or the alternation of intense, vibrating shopping areas and disciplined public squares can express meaning in and through their connections.

A new art form of our century is the collage, a device by which materials from the most heterogeneous fields are brought into a contrasting but complementing ensemble. The cityscape is to some degree a counterpart of the collage, in which the contrast and variety of the elements produces a vitality through tension and the potential of structure. Through the cooperation of architects, designers, painters, and sculptors skilled in the expressive nature of forms, a wealth of new architectural devices, color, and textural values can be brought into play. We must learn to make every building expressive, not just by its material and structural principles, but by the nature of the life it serves. Secure on this level of small units, the next step would be to group the buildings where the spatial relations with each other and with the ground could form a broader scale of differentiation by means of a common spirit. The individuality of a building should cooperate with the expressive form of a group of buildings. This expressive articulation of the cityscape can be expanded to include districts, areas, and sections. By defining characteristic features, the variety that exists latently can be made manifest. Redirecting interest toward differentiation would inevitably bring qualities of visual distinction to the fore.

If the spatial network of a city is logical and its physical patterning clear and legible, then the people will be able to perform their complex activities efficiently. There is a threshold beyond which social intercourse becomes impossible. Our simple perceptual processes select and edit the complex visual field until a meaningful hierarchy of significant shapes arises. Similarly, in the intricate pattern of group communication in an extended environment there is a need to break up the complex field into distinct groups and units and then relate them in a functional and logical pattern. The bigger the city area, the greater the need to make the component parts (buildings, streets, districts) distinct in character and with clearly defined boundaries. They must be sensed not only in their individual characteristics but as a part of the over-all background pattern. The individuality of a group or unit must also be realized in its functional connectedness with the social, economic, and cultural whole of the city. Thus, the physical makeup of the urban environment must not only take the individual units into consideration, but these distinctly perceived separate features must also be grasped in their relation to the spatial and functional fibers of the whole.

The increasing differentiation of the city offers a wide variety of scenes. Each city possesses a total personality, yet it contains a broad spectrum of individually characteristic units. The increasing scope of the living space of a city brings a greater variety of stimulation, opportunities, and vistas to explore and exploit. If the city can be structured and unified, therefore, the increase in complexity becomes an asset. No richness is added, however, through the mere multiplication of identical units or areas. Only a disciplined differentiation of the city offers perceptual challenges such as contribute to a city environment that is emotionally and intellectually stimulating. The difference between the impact of continuous challenge on the mechanical and on the organic level is clearly put in a phrase from D'Arcy Thompson: "The soles of our shoes wear thin through use, but the soles of our feet become strong through it." The challenge created by the wide range of stimulations coming from a well-differentiated and at the same time well-articulated environment is an important factor in the growth of knowledge, in richness of experience, and in civic connectedness.

Differentiation must be purposeful. The variation in character among city areas has to be consistent with realities; otherwise articulation becomes tiresome repetition. Extreme contrasts—for example, the contrast between a wealthy residential and an impoverished slum area—defy articulation because of a gap too wide for bridging and they attenuate the potential unity of the city. But open squares, narrow streets, a tranquil park, a business area, or a well-sheltered residential section—all are perceived more clearly, more intensely, and more characteristically if they are in proper proportion to one another in size and distance, and in proper order in the sequential circulation pattern of the city. In any artistic creation, varied elements have to be brought to a common goal. A city must find a structure in which a wide range of elements is brought into a common functioning whole through gradations, contrasting boundaries, rhythmically repeated similarities. A well-harmonized basic spatial pattern can be greatly helpful in manipulating group life, mixing people, or keeping them separated, as necessary. At the same time, however, it is imperative that this pattern be flexible enough to permit new orientation via improved technology, changes in custom, and new groupings.

A city form that has such unity does more than facilitate the life within it. The richness, inner logic, and harmony of units in an urban environment function symbolically. In a certain sense, there arises an artistic creation that stimulates sensibilities, increases sensitivity to surroundings, and transforms attitudes.

ARTICULATING THE CITY: THE PROCESS

Every process of high-level schematization follows this sequence. (1) The introduction of stress into the unstructured field yields a figural pattern. (2) Component units of the figural pattern are read through the establishment of their boundaries; we become aware of the parts of the structure. (3) The connexity of the parts is read through the determination of the links among them. (4) The structure itself is read through integrating the parts in their connexity. Thus, the low-level structure of the field becomes a high-level structure.

We bring the symbolic structure of the urban environment into legibility according to the following sequence. (1) From the perceptual field of the urban environment we resolve such units as houses, streets, squares, neighborhoods, sections, according to our grasp of the individuality of their features. (2) We read the boundaries—rivers, walls, gaps, changes of form or expression—that define these units. Thus we become aware of the parts of the city structure. (3) We read the connexity of the parts in terms of their bonds and links—on the one hand, the traffic arteries and rail and transit lines that collect and distribute the life blood of the city; on the other, doors, windows, bridges, tunnels, and long inclusive vistas. (4) The parts in their connexity are read together as a common structure—the symbolic form, the intrinsic symbol of the urban whole.

The "New-Yorkness" of New York is due largely to the exciting variety of its constituent areas. Fifth Avenue, Central Park, the United Nations building, Harlem, Greenwich Village, the East River, Wall Street, etc., together make up what we perceive as New York the city. In our imagination we may toy with the idea of leaving out one or another of these areas, thus changing the composite character of New York. To test our sense of the wholeness of the city, we may carry the game further and in our imagination gradually delete a series of successive parts. It soon becomes evident that eliminating certain parts of New York implies not only a change of size but a change of character. If we played the same game with a city like Los Angeles, whose parts are less differentiated, the deletion of some of them would mean more of a change in size than in character. We may carry on this imaginary game in another direction: instead of leaving out parts, we can try relocating them. We will inevitably discover a certain logic of growth expressed by the present structural configuration. Evidently, the variety of characteristic areas is an integral part of New York. The boundaries between one and another region are consequent and belong to its structural expressiveness.

The communication path has less symbolic significance, for recent years have witnessed major transformations without altering the essential characteristics of the metropolitan whole. Many smaller cities, however, have resisted the passage of new throughways bypassing the center of the city, for this would entail not only an economic displacement but also a major shift in expressive character.

In the town small enough to be grasped in a clear structural pattern, the communication and transportation network tells us the most. The larger the city, the more significant the differentiation of its parts, their boundaries, and connecting links. On a visual level, the transportation network as a whole becomes increasingly conceptual, a question of cartography abstracted from immediate visual legibility. Nevertheless, key parts of the transportation network can become symbolic through their autographic style: bridges, stations, or other details. A bus stop in Boston is marked by a band on a pole, in New York by a sidewalk standard. A Metro entrance with its *art-nouveau* character means Paris. Trolleys run in subway tubes only in Boston. The Moscow subway station is *sui generis*. The door does not open automatically in the London underground; you must open it yourself.

Differences in age further enrich the characterizing parts. In, let us say, a small New England town composed largely of historically meaningful buildings, a few new buildings may provide too sudden a contrast, and, instead of adding to the total, may have a jarring effect. In a large metropolis, where historic growth has characteristic areas comparable to the age rings of a tree, each new one is absorbed in a visually and meaningfully connected continuum and adds to the richness of the whole. The new buildings or sections have no formal structural connections with the total but complement one another in an enriching sense. The Lever Brothers building or the United Nations building in New York may bring a shift of emphasis but always within the total field. On the other hand, the John Hancock building in Boston is too abrupt a contrast to the smaller scale of its surroundings and is thus a disturbing and unbalanced factor. Philadelphia, like Boston, abounding in visible links connecting the modern supercity with its eighteenth- and early nineteenth-century past, has developed a master plan for ensuring the survival of these historic links in the symbolic patterning of the burgeoning metropolis.

ARTICULATING THE CITY: THE CONNECTIONS

The door, the window, or any opening between enclosed spatial units is an index to the freedom of movement possible on the actual physical level, to the freedom of the eye to wander on the visual level. There are numerous devices men have discovered or invented that bridge separate, bounded spatial regions.

The window or the door has another important feature as well: it can be regulated, that is, it can be a part of the fence or barrier when it is closed, or it can function on its own terms when it acts as an opening. The height, the width, the strength, the degree of opening are also indexes of the opportunities for freedom of traffic. The link or path between spatially defined areas helps to articulate a spatial continuum. This may be an extended door or window providing a direct transition from one place to another; it may be an extended transition actually incorporating spatial areas. Roads, bridges, tunnels, air routes, river paths, subways, overpasses, underpasses, rotaries, or cloverleafs are such patterns; they connect regions by concentrating and distributing traffic. Utilities and communications have corresponding distribution paths: power lines, water pipes, telegraph and telephone lines, radio and television channels. Here again, the visible features are the indexes of certain actual or potential events in transportation or communication. They may have a wide range of spatial configuration in different geometries.

Boundaries, openings, and links are important aspects of the intrinsic symbolism of the urban environment. Their specific characters, their esthetic features, their references to the life pattern—all constitute important elements of the symbolic structure. The degrees of relationship between boundaries and openings are determined by the type of life associated with them and are expressive of the values and aspirations of the group. The differences between a well-fenced suburban area and an unfenced fluid space show clear differences in human attitudes. A confining, restrained subdivision of space expresses a lack of a sense of community in a typical class, a caste, or a prestige group. Condensed space, without rigid isolation devices, facilitates and expresses aspects of community life.

As we have said above, single factors become intrinsic symbols only through their structural connectedness. Naturally, these spatial devices gain meaning only through reference to what they divide or connect. The boundaries are boundaries of characteristic spatial areas. The interior of a house and the garden outside are particular types of surroundings; their dividing boundaries are meaningful only in terms of what they separate. Today, there is a growing tendency to design houses in which the boundaries between the inside and the outside are minimized. Structural devices of the house accent the structure of the outside, for example, walls that extend into the garden. On the other hand, landscape elements assume an important role inside the building.

This semi-fusion of two distinct spatial atmospheres is justified for many reasons. As technical knowledge enabled the production of buildings with thermal and illumination control, the old heavy-masonry protective walls became unnecessary in order to give a feeling of shelter. On the other hand, as the increasingly mechanized world isolated us from the rich fluctuation of the organic world, the psychological need arose to borrow as much as possible from nature to make urban life acceptable. Here again, the structural combinations of the space areas, with their defining or connecting devices, are characteristic of the needs, attitudes, and values of contemporary man. In the broader urban pattern, similar needs may be recognized. The city is no longer an enclosed territory with walls to protect it from an outside enemy. It is a spatial pattern that needs to fight against the internal enemy of complete isolation from fresh air, sunshine, and open space. Boundaries, connecting links, and openings are being structured in a new pattern. This structure is again a symbolic form expressing certain emerging values.

TRAFFIC AND SYMBOLIC FORM

Traffic is a major battleground of the city's struggle to preserve itself as a place where the human life within it may continue to exist, to grow, and to encompass its organic and symbolic ends. Traffic and the parking of vehicles are a factor of confusion in our attempts to articulate the city form.

There is a basic form relation among those stable elements in the environment that have long historic memories and relatively well-established esthetic roles. Though our spatial concepts and our dominant esthetic attitudes have undergone changes, we have accumulated knowledge of what the satisfactory space patterns of related spatial forms are. We have, however, little historic guidance for relating static space forms, such as buildings, with today's fast-moving vehicles of transportation.

Problems arise at many levels. First of all, the aggressive dynamics must be balanced by the larger stable world. It would also seem that there is an incompatible contrast between the forms of buildings and of cars. This is most apparent whenever the cars are stationary and their endless line blurs the perceptual ordering of architectural relationships. The clash of colors of the two- and three-tone cars, with their chaotic geometry and chromium haloes, serves only to create disturbance. Herein lies one of the most serious esthetic bottlenecks of the urban scene. In motion cars tend to blend into a kaleidoscopic stream that, in an esthetic sense, can accent the nature of the surrounding buildings. Standing, they at best compete with and in most cases suffocate their surroundings.

Aside from functional needs, the esthetic handicap alone is serious enough to demand our attention. Few of the innumer-

able parking solutions take this factor into consideration.
Although fringe parking alleviates the downtown traffic press,
it takes unpleasant visual forms in the important connecting
areas between downtown and the city periphery. The problem
of desk-side parking facilities for new office buildings, theaters,
hospitals, and stores will be fully solved only when the esthetic
aspect is controlled. This will necessitate some carefully considered, visually satisfactory screens to hide the groupings of
motor cars. Natural or artificial screening, such as trees or
esthetically pleasing fences, will help to accommodate the
appearance of parking lots and meter areas to the surrounding
city scene. Municipal or private garages, in alleviating parking,
must, like open-air lots, be considered as to their location, their
approaches, and their visual relations to the total space pattern. Open-deck, exposed-steel garages can bring a new technical accent to the environment in keeping with the car forms.

The filling station is a similar problem. Its gaudy, attention-
catching "acrobatic" devices in a sense are justified by the
necessity of attracting the fast-moving eye, but the station, too,
must find a proper relation with its background.

Both the problem of advertising and display and that of
parking demand a thorough analysis and fundamental proposals. These fields are allied through their visual needs. Each
has arrived at a point of supersaturation at which original purposes have been lost through exaggerated crowding. Both
problems demand a new structural solution, common denomi-
nators that can reduce their complexity into controllable terms.
A possible starting point is to eliminate all unnecessary redun-
dancy in an attempt to simplify a codification of the elements.
This need is already self-evident in advertising. Parking simpli-
fication can be achieved by concealing those aspects of the environment that choke off visual and physical traffic orientation.

This system of codification has two interdependent objectives: to be functionally efficient and esthetically satisfactory.
Both goals are important in a broader context, for they must
be related to and fit in with their surroundings. There is no

rigidly fixed code one can use, for the underlying objective in designing an efficient communication system is to make it an esthetically pleasing, vital form with flexibility and susceptibility to change.

LIGHT

Today, the visual manifestations of the urban world are greatly modified through the use of artificial lights. Spatial forms and their interrelations are overlaid with a different type of pattern because of illumination at night, and the city has more than ever a double life.

Both the problem of orientation and the problems of continuity are fundamentally transformed when day changes to night. Cues that are legible in the daytime become largely useless at night. Forms, colors, and distances that by day may have a satisfactory esthetic configuration are considerably transformed by the lights, which usually have little to do with the surfaces, edges, and consequent form relationships of the daylight hours.

Since the city as a physical object that we perceive remains constant during this double life, it is important to understand the problems of continuity in this particular transformation. Few people would deny that it is a rewarding esthetic experience to perceive the first stages of transformation at dusk. In this first phase, the major forms and spaces of the cityscape are still clearly indicated, but a new system of space is superimposed on this form world through the change of the dark window holes into bright sparks of electric light. Streets once marked by the boundaries of buildings receive their new outlines in street lights. The multicolored traffic is gradually transformed into the mobile illumination traces of the cars.

As yet, a conscious exploitation of the inherent possibilities of these changes has hardly been attempted. There are many promising possibilities. Because of its wide range of intensity and color, illumination can be utilized as an important device for guiding orientation. Without sacrificing their primary role of illuminating, street lights could be carefully modified in position and color to synchronize with the coding of location and direction.

The incredibly rich esthetic potentials of the new range of colors, their shapes and their brightness as they are offered to us by the new tools of illumination, are the potential palettes of a new civic art. It is not difficult to imagine what such purposeful efforts could achieve, for, through lucky accidents, we have some amazing examples in which the accidental configurations of display lights combined with the car lights produce visions of great splendor.

In a certain sense the forms of modern architecture and the very existence of the present scale of urban life stem from advances in illumination. The transmission of light—natural and artificial—through large sheets of glass has been decisive in the development of a new sense of space and a new awareness of lighted structures. Without artificial lighting in our houses and on our streets, we could not orient ourselves, and the circulation of our goods and our persons would diminish to a comparative trickle. All twenty-four hours of the day are now exploitable, and nature's sharp articulation of night and day has in our cities fused into a single day-night fabric of time. Moreover, no matter how chaotic, blighted, or illegible a city is, it is transformed when evening comes and the lights go on. Points, lines, plane figures, and volumes of light—steady and winking, moving and still, white and colored—from windows, signs, spectaculars, headlights, traffic lights, street lights, combine into a fluid, luminous wonder—one of the great sights of this or any age. This impressive sight is a byproduct of utility, an accident if you will, but its accidental wealth reminds us of the concentrated, ordered beauty of the great windows of thirteenth-century cathedrals.

What has been said previously about the periodicity between orderly and random patterning holds true here as well. The major poles in this context are darkness and light. It is a commonplace experience to have a strong response when moving from a dark unlit side street to a gaudy theater district. But there are innumerable gradations of experience between these two extremes. The utilization of such qualities of experience as such transitions evoke could create a new type of patterning of the urban night scene. The contrast and transition gained by regulating the brightness of illumination and locating light sources through varying their heights and intervals could give both articulation and enrichment. A focused source of light, such as a candle, a lamp, or a fireplace, generates a focused attention, almost a feeling of warmth or nesting. Our interests are so function-centered that such emotional use of light is rarely given thought. There is a growing interest in developing a new meaning and a new form to city cores. A carefully devised ordering of light could become an important tool in drawing people together in certain areas.

Light is now used for the dramatic emphasis of major buildings. This emphasis could be carried into a broader scope, defining the boundaries of city scenes, indicating characteristic differences, and accenting the most important foci of common life.

The great need is to bring the isolated accidental effects into a coordinated sequential pattern in which the individual features mutually define one another by contrasting accents of their unique qualities. It is also important to create a common, continuous night scene that corresponds on its own terms to the structural, spatial, and living aspects of the urban reality.

At the moment, almost all work connected with the lighting of cities is done by illumination engineers or by advertising-display specialists. Each of them takes on a task with his limited horizon, utterly disregarding the implications of his own work for the adjacent areas or for the problems to which his work gives rise. A new type of creative mentality is needed, one that can combine knowledge of the craft with heightened esthetic sensibility and greater awareness of the problems of the city.

The utilization of climatic changes in the surrounding world belongs to this area of thinking. It is evident that the cityscape undergoes major transformations during the day through the changing patterns of light and shadow. In our speed-obsessed, fast-growing cities, there is little use of the important factor of shadow change. Here again, the consciously planned act has little value, but a careful analysis of the esthetic implications of changing shadows in certain significant areas could help plot changes that are in tune with the richness inherent in the relationship of light, shadow, and form.

The use of light to clarify and inform architectural spaces and complex cityscapes is not yet a discipline. We have no command of creative principles based upon a thorough understanding of light and the tools of lighting and upon a full awareness of what is needed to raise the art of employing light to a high level. Certain preliminary steps have been taken. We know, for instance, how to make illumination sufficient and comfortable. This has been the goal of illumination engineers, who have learned all that physiology and physics can teach them in this respect, both in natural and in artificial lighting.

Architects and city planners want more than comfort and amplitude in lighting. They know that they have great opportunities in designing with light, for stainless steel, reinforced concrete, and new structural systems are fitting partners for lighting tools and, with them, suggest a whole new range of light qualities for architectural surfaces and spaces. But they do not know how to take full advantage of their opportunities. No doubt their capacity will grow as they continue to deal with the problem, but a major breakthrough seems hardly in the offing. It is possible, however, that such a breakthrough could be at least hastened through an effort that is not directed toward the immediate problems of architecture and planning but toward the exploration of the realm of lighting itself as a field for artistic expression and the creative imagination.

By joining territories presently unconnected into a common

realm of the use of light, we can hope for the development of fundamentally new principles based upon the full mobilization of artistic sensibilities and a full grasp of technical knowledge. All of our experience leads us to believe that there is a higher unity among the great traditional systems of working with light: the twelfth- and thirteenth-century glass techniques of York, Chartres, Bourges, Le Mans, Sens, Laon and the Sainte-Chapelle; the vibrating play of light of the Ravenna glass mosaics; the sculptural modulation of simple buildings in the Mediterranean region, from ancient times to the present, with their unsurpassed exploitation of sunlight to define form and enhance surface; and, finally, the use of light in modern stage-craft, still photography and movies, display, the electronic instrumentation of light, the projected play of light, electronically controlled lighting devices. Their common principles must be discovered and applied in important tasks.

The imaginative use of light is the neglected area of modern design. In other areas, architects, planners, engineers, and artists have established the basis for a physical environment impressive in scale, authentic in its solution of twentieth-century needs, and promising in its enrichment of our life. Technical advances in lighting have taken place, and designers with light have had their victories. Nevertheless, lighting can be developed in ways we have not even begun to explore, and an undreamed-of opulence of esthetic experience awaits us.

TEXTURE AND RHYTHM

We have found that periodicity is an important factor in the perceptual structuring of our visual environment. Complex scenes, high buildings, high-intensity and low-intensity lighting, closed and open spaces are elements that recur. The recurrence of visual features in a structured sequence produces a textural rhythm that facilitates perceptual unification of the form of the city.

Abrupt change and gradual change are the two basic units

of periodic modulation. For example, the angles of streets may change in unison, bringing rhythmic order. Similarly, a gradual diminution or increase of the height of buildings, the width of streets, and the flow of traffic organizes a directional structure.

Total regularity is taxing to the human organism and has functional as well as esthetic shortcomings. Initial steps in planning parkways (abandoned in the current design of throughways) were taken to avoid changes in direction, to adjust speed to a constant rate, and to frame the roadway with standardized buildings and landscaping. The monotony of a long trip over one of these turnpikes is not only psychologically displeasing but dangerous as well. The urban environment, on the other hand, suffers more from the dangers of overcomplexity than from those of monotony.

Textures as qualities of living surface are significant in the rhythmic structuring of the cityscape. In a complex environment like ours, the architectural spatial order is becoming less and less dominant and the textural play of buildings in sequence increasingly noticeable. To bring the vibrating, changing surfaces into a perceivable order, certain regularities among them have to be emphasized. One is the grain or density; another is the inherent direction. In the esthetic organization of the urban scene, both aspects of texture can be utilized. Regular changes from finely to coarsely grained surface textures bring their own type of order. The direction of textural qualities can best be illustrated by simple examples. When seen from a distance, roof patterns whether made from tile or shingle vary in their apparent directional alignment according to the movement of the eye, thus producing an oscillating surface texture. A tree whose leaves are wavering before a brick wall shows two textural surfaces, different both in grain and in mobility. The flutter of the leaves is important to the esthetic quality perceived.

Our city scenes are made up of a rich combination of such textural characteristics; stable and mobile textures with different intensities and different directions are woven into a common fabric. At this moment, all the threads are accidental and, in an esthetic sense, uncontrolled. Although there is very little chance to control completely the textural range of the environment, an awareness of some of its effects could be a guide to those who are charged with the tasks of city planning.

There are many natural visual experiences that are esthetically pleasing mainly because of their periodicity: the rhythmic oscillation of waves; the modulation of flames in a fireplace; the repeated patterns of light and shadow everywhere. The regular repetition of action and repose is the key to every rhythm of work or esthetic process.

In our performance of so complex a task as the perception of our urban environment, periodicity has more intricate aspects. It combines regularly repeated configurations, such as dense traffic or arrangements of park benches. Part of the great richness of the Paris scene is owed to the large number of small parks recurring at almost regular intervals. As activity must be punctuated by repose, so should the task of orientation be balanced by frequently recurrent opportunities for rest. In traveling through the urban environment there are a great number of periodic lulls such as traffic lights or bus stops. These directly underscore the rhythmic structure of the environment.

It is important to have a variety of situations each with its rhythmic character, contrasting with one another, flowing into one another. The vitality of the cityscape depends on this. It is significant that some of the most sensitive and daring painters of our age have been occupied in reading and expressing the rhythm of the urban scene. Mondrian, one of the major figures in contemporary art, is obsessed with expressing the rhythmic richness of the metropolis. His *Broadway Boogie-Woogie,* a major opus of twentieth-century art, draws its stimulation and its expressive idiom from the pulsation of New York city traffic according to the beats and measures of streets and buildings.

The amplitude and frequency of the images reaching us

may be interpreted in terms of thresholds. As we have pointed out above, the human capacity for perception is limited by certain physiological and psychological factors. We must close our eyes when we look into the extreme brightness of the sun. There is a definite limit to the number of elements we can instantaneously perceive with clarity. Beyond a certain speed, changing signals cannot be grasped individually, for the impression fuses into a blur.

These delimiting thresholds can derive either from the motion of the observer or from the velocity of the objects or patterns in the environment, and they determine whether there is to be order or disorder in continuous visual experiences. The frequency factor is the more dominant one here. Because of the threshold in our perceptual capacity, only certain limited impacts when we pass through a city scene can be retained and interpreted.

Some thresholds we ourselves establish through immediate purpose, or else have established long ago through our becoming sensitive or resistant to qualities of the environment. There are some absolute thresholds, however. Objects close to us when we are on a speeding train, for example, are perceived as a blur, and we are unable to resolve clear forms.

In the total pattern of perception, both clear and distorted vision are esthetically important. A continuous chain of clear information may force us to break our attention if it does not give the necessary periodicity to the process of perception. Without the succession of activity and repose in our perception, the scene would be so dense with information that it would lie beyond our grasp. A world made continually illegible by overcomplexity or an extreme speed of impacts strains and irritates the observer. Artistic forms employ a periodicity of order and disorder to build up a total continuity through the proper sequence of these relationships.

In the urban scene, the sequences of a consciously planned pattern are impossible, but a modification of extremes and a timing of certain aspects of the poles of order and disorder could be accomplished. For instance, the monotony of a regularly patterned city space can be interrupted by a condensed shopping area, full of variety and extreme in complexity and tempo. Conversely, the complex dense atmosphere of some urban centers can be broken by small squares of patterned landscape. It will require an increased sensibility to make such conscious changes.

In its processes of growth, the city goes through these phases of unstructured randomness and patterned orderliness. Only after a certain stage of structuring and activity does it become necessary to interconnect them in a planned, logical fashion. After reaching the ordered stage, the city will branch out again in new directions of growth, introducing uncontrolled vistas, full of challenge and complexity. By clearly understanding the interconnection between city growth and our perceptual processes, we may find some guiding principles for regulating the evolution of the city.

11. The American Intellectual Versus the American City

MORTON and LUCIA WHITE

ALTHOUGH THE CITY has become one of the most absorbing and most intensively studied social problems in America today, and although it is now fashionable for intellectuals to express an almost tender concern for its future, to hope that its decay can be arrested, and to offer plans for its revitalization, this has not always been the attitude of our greatest American thinkers.[1] For a variety of reasons they have expressed different degrees of hostility toward urban life in America, hostility which may be partly responsible for a feeling on the part of today's city planner and urban reformer that he has no mythology or mystique on which he can rest or depend. We have no tradition of romantic attachment to the city in our highbrow literature, nothing that remotely resembles the Greek philosopher's attachment to the *polis* or the French writer's affection for Paris. And this fits very well with the frequently defended thesis that the American writer has been more than usually alienated from the society in which he lives, that he is typically in revolt against it. Throughout the nineteenth century our society was becoming more and more urbanized, but the literary tendency to denigrate the American city hardly declined in proportion. If anything, it increased in intensity.

Faced with this fact about the history of American thought, the contemporary student of the city can take one of two opposing attitudes. He, at his peril, can turn his back on the tradition of Jefferson, Emerson, Thoreau, Hawthorne, Melville, Poe, Henry Adams, Henry James, Louis Sullivan, Frank Lloyd Wright, and John Dewey. In this case he will treat some of the American city's profoundest critics as irresponsible literary men or as idle metaphysicians who fled the city rather than face its problems. Or he can regard this critical tradition as a repository of deep, though troubling, wisdom, one which raises basic questions for any urban reformer, partly because its premonitions and fears have been more than justified by the passage of time. There is no doubt that the second is the wiser course. He who would improve the American city can only profit by an awareness of what some of our greatest minds have said, felt, and thought about one of the most conspicuous and most troubling features of our national life.

One cannot deny, of course, that there were pro-urban literary voices like Whitman's, or that there were urban sociologists like Robert Park who tried to speak up for the city. But they are voices in "the city wilderness," never comparing in volume with the anti-urban roar in the national literary pantheon. The urbanist must face the fact that the anti-urbanist does not live only in the Kentucky hills, in the Rockies, in the Ozarks, in the Cracker country, or the bayous. He lives in the mind and heart of America as conceived by the intellectual historian. The intellect, whose home is the city, according to some sociologists, has been the American city's sharpest critic. Everyone knows that Jefferson once hoped to discourage the development of the city in America, but he was only the first of a long and varied list of critics of the city.

Jefferson despised the manners and principles of the urban "mob" as he knew it in Europe and he hoped to keep it from crossing the Atlantic intact. He certainly did not think of the city as "The Hope of Democracy," as some Progressive theorists did at the turn of the twentieth century. He adopted a conciliatory tone about the city in his old age when he said in 1816 that we could not possibly depend on England for manufactures, as he had originally thought, and therefore we *needed* cities. But this does not show any *love* for the city. The country and its yeomen Jefferson loved all his life; in his old age he grudgingly accepted the manufacturing city as a necessity.

The same War of 1812 which led Jefferson to reassess his views was followed by a great expansion of the American city. It inaugurated a major phase of urban civilization between the Revolution and the Civil War. By 1860 the urban population was eleven times what it had been in 1820. The early decades of the nineteenth century saw the decline of Jefferson's empiricism among American intellectuals, and the emergence of philosophical Transcendentalism, but a distaste for the city persisted among American writers.

The growth of the city in the North produced an even sharper reaction in Ralph Waldo Emerson than the European city had produced in Jefferson. Emerson's first philosophical work, *Nature,* appeared in 1836, in the middle of that interval which witnessed an eleven-fold increase in our urban population. Its very title was a protest against what he thought was happening. Partly under the influence of English romanticism, Emerson and some of his friends took to deprecating manufacture, art, and civilization, and so it was not long before they took to criticizing the city, the greatest of artifacts. The distaste for the city as an artificial creation was associated in Emerson's mind, as it was in the case of many romantic thinkers, with doubts about the value of science as an avenue to truth. And yet Emerson agreed with the scientifically minded Jefferson about the nasty manners and principles of the city. Whereas Jefferson was given to arguing the defects of the city in common-sense political terms, Emerson sought to buttress his feelings by a metaphysical theory. Hence we may label his period as the metaphysical period of anti-urbanism. To be is to be natural for Emerson. In the wilderness he said he found "something more dear and connate than in streets or villages." The life of the city was "artificial and curtailed"; it destroyed solitude, poetry, and philosophy.

One will find passages in which Emerson extolled the appli-

cation of science and the virtues of civilization, the need for
sociability to educate a man's sympathies, and the advantages
of specialization that allow each man to develop his own
talents. This suggests a more friendly view of the industrial
urban society which was emerging in his own lifetime. But he
always harped on the human failings of State Street and com-
mercialism. At times Emerson could celebrate the artifice of
pure technology, but he persistently attacked the debasement
of moral standards by those who pursued nothing but wealth
in the cities as he knew them. One is reminded of Thorstein
Veblen's praise of urban industry even as he attacked its financial captains, for it was Veblen who saw the modern industrial
city as the *locus classicus* of conspicuous waste.

Thoreau went even farther than Emerson in his distaste for
civilization and the city, for Thoreau also attacked the village
and the farm. *Walden* is a bible of anti-urbanism, in which
Thoreau celebrates the life of the isolated individual, living in
Nature and free of *all* social attachments. No wonder that
Thoreau refused to visit the Saturday Club, which provided
one of the few values of Boston in Emerson's eyes: intellectual
conversation. And when Thoreau refused, Perry Miller reminds
us, he put his refusal in no uncertain terms: "The only room
in Boston which I visit with alacrity is the Gentlemen's Room
at the Fitchburg Depot, where I wait for cars, sometimes for
two hours, in order to get out of town."[2] No wonder Henry
James said that Thoreau "was essentially a sylvan personage."[3]

If Jefferson attacked the city on political grounds, and if
Emerson and Thoreau may be represented as criticizing it
from the point of view of transcendental metaphysics, what
shall we say of Poe, Hawthorne, and Melville, all of whom may
be added to our list of pre-Civil War critics of the city? They
were far from political theorists or metaphysicians but all of
them saw the city as the scene of sin and crime. Speaking of
them, Harry Levin says: "For our dreamers, America was a
garden, an agrarian Eden, which was losing its innocence by
becoming citified. Melville had located his City of Woe in

London or Liverpool; Poe had tracked down imaginary crimes in the streets of an imagined Paris; and Hawthorne had exposed sins most luridly among the ruins of Rome."[4] As in Jefferson's case, the urban models of extreme crime and sinfulness were not located in the United States by most of our pre-Civil War anti-urbanists, but they saw dark omens in the streets of American cities which made them fear that they might become like Paris, London, Liverpool, or Rome.

The observant de Tocqueville expressed his worry about the American city in 1835, one year before Emerson's essay *Nature* appeared. He said that the fact that America as yet had no dominating metropolis was one of those circumstances which tended to maintain a democratic republic in the United States and to counteract that great danger to which all democracies are subject—the tyranny of the majority. But de Tocqueville thought that the "lower ranks" which inhabited Philadelphia (pop. 161,000) and New York (pop. 202,000) in the 1830's "constitute a rabble even more formidable than the populace of European towns. They consist of freed blacks . . . who are condemned by the laws and by public opinion to a hereditary state of misery and degradation. They also contain a multitude of Europeans who have been driven to the shore of the New World by their misfortunes or their misconduct; and they bring to the United States all our greatest vices, without any of those interests which counteract their baneful influence. As inhabitants of a country where they have no civil rights, they are ready to turn all the passions which agitate the community to their own advantage; thus, within the last few months, serious riots have broken out in Philadelphia and New York."[5] So seriously did de Tocqueville treat this matter that he said: "I look upon the size of certain American cities, and especially on the nature of their population, as a real danger which threatens the future security of the democratic republics of the New World; and I venture to predict that they will perish from this circumstance, unless the government succeeds in creating an armed force which, while it remains under the

control of the majority of the nation, will be independent of
the town population and able to repress its excesses."[6]

If this could be the conclusion of the most astute foreign
observer ever to visit our shores, it is not surprising that some
of our great literary figures might have developed less than an
admiring view of our urban culture between the Revolution
and the Civil War. Optimistic empiricists like Jefferson, optimistic transcendentalists like Emerson, pessimistic believers in
original sin like Hawthorne and Melville, all forgot their philosophical differences when they looked upon the American city,
even before it developed into the industrial jungle it was to
become between the Civil War and the end of the nineteenth
century.

Between 1860 and 1900 the urban population quadrupled
while the rural population only doubled; and, what is more
staggering and significant, between 1790 and 1890, while the
total population of the country increased sixteen times, the
urban population increased 139 times.[7] The great exodus from
the countryside was in full force, and New England became
the scene of deserted hill and village farms, while the city's
problems became the great social problems of the nation. The
city became the home of the elevated railroad, the trolley car,
the cable car, the subway, the apartment house, the telephone,
and the skyscraper, while it continued to encourage what one
physician called "American nervousness."

Among the most influential and most fastidious observers of
this development were Henry Adams and the younger Henry
James. Both were men of literary genius, both were members
of cultivated families with wealth in their backgrounds, and
for both of them the American city provided a profound spiritual problem. Because Henry Adams and Henry James lived
in the age of the city's supremacy, they did not speak of it, as
Jefferson had, as a remote future phenomenon or as something
existing in Europe alone. And, unlike Thoreau, they did not
feel as though they had only the American city and the American wilderness to choose between. Adams and James were

both refined, civilized, indeed urban men whose animadversions on the American city are made more significant precisely because they were not opposed to cities in principle. They demonstrate what a hard time the American city had at the hands of nineteenth-century intellectuals. For here at last were two *city* types who also found the American city sadly wanting. Their reaction to the American city is more esthetic, more literary, more psychological than that of their predecessors Jefferson and Emerson.

The two most important documents for an understanding of the views of Adams and James are the former's *Education* and the latter's *The American Scene*. It is significant that the great problem of *The Education of Henry Adams* was to steer a course between the poles of town and country, between the Boston and Quincy of his childhood. "Town," Adams tells us, "was restraint, law, unity. Country, only seven miles away, was liberty, diversity, outlawry, the endless delight of mere sense impressions given by nature for nothing, and breathed by boys without knowing it."[8] Adams also tells us that he spent his life trying to choose between the ways of life they represented, without ever making up his mind. And yet, in a sense, he did make up his mind, or the social forces of America made it up for him. He could not go back to the Quincy house of his grandfather Adams. And, being no Thoreau, he had to live in the American city if he was to live anywhere in America. But what was *the* American city in his mature years? Surely not Boston, but New York. And when Henry Adams looked at the New York of 1868, he tells us in a book which he wrote in 1905 that he felt swept aside by the forces pushing the country in a new direction. "His world," he lamented, "was dead. Not a Polish Jew fresh from Warsaw or Cracow—not a furtive Yaccob or Ysaac still reeking of the Ghetto, snarling a weird Yiddish to the officers of the customs—but had a keener instinct, and intenser energy, and a freer hand than he—American of Americans, with Heaven knew how many Puritans and Patriots behind him, and an education that had cost a civil war."[9] Adams felt like the dispossessed Indian and the buffalo in America after 1865, for it was a banker's, and neither a buffalo's nor a Bostonian's, world. To Henry Adams, New York symbolized the spiritual confusion of America at the end of the nineteenth century.

Henry James, as one might expect, also complained about his birthplace, New York, after a period of flirtation with it. James attacked it most explicitly in *The American Scene,* published in 1907 as the report of an expatriate revisiting the country of his birth. He, too, spoke of the city's chaos, and even the New York skyline insulted his very expressively complex sensibilities. He complained of the lack of history and of the lack of time for history in a way that reminds one of his early critical work on Nathaniel Hawthorne. The buildings, he said, "never speak to you, in the manner of the builded majesties of the world . . . towers, or temples, or fortresses or palaces with the authority of things of permanence or even of things of long duration."[10] History had given way to commerce: "The great city is projected into its future as practically a huge continuous fifty-floored conspiracy against the very idea of the ancient graces."[11] The city lacked order, structure, dignity, history. James speaks of it as "a heaped industrial battlefield" and as a scene of "the universal will to move—to move, move, move, as an end in itself, an appetite at any price."[12] He missed what he called "organic social relations,"[13] and he felt some pleasurable relief when he visited Philadelphia, because it didn't "bristle," and because "it went back."[14] In this spirit he warned: "Let not the unwary . . . visit Ellis Island"[15] as Henry Adams might have warned in *his* snobbish way. James was upset by what he called "that loud primary stage of alienism which New York most offers to sight."[16] And he dreamed "of the luxury of some such close and sweet and *whole* national consciousness as that of the Switzer and the Scot."[17] His final head-shaking conclusion was "that there was no escape from the ubiquitous alien into the future or even into the present; there was no escape but into the past."[18]

Of course, one must not forget that Henry James was a cosmopolite, a life-long inhabitant of cities, a man who is reputed to have dined out more than any resident of London in his day. One must be mindful of the fact that his novel *The Princess Casamassima* represents an effort to penetrate the depths of London, as does his famous admiring essay on that city. But James viewed the *American* city in an entirely different way. After his harsh handling of the Boston reformers in *The Bostonians*, the American city did not provide him with any serious material for a full-length novel because he found neither the uptown nor the downtown of the American city sufficiently interesting, as F. O. Mathiessen has pointed out.[19] And even *The Princess Casamassima* shows a greater interest in the bizarre doings of weirdly inspired misfits and aristocrats, whose philanthropic concern with the slums James satirizes, than a sustained interest in the typical life of London. With characteristic delicacy and insight he saw the crushing, oppressive defects of the British metropolis of his day, but he could never bring himself to the same kind of sympathetic concern with the American metropolis that we find in Dreiser, Crane, or Norris.

Although we are primarily concerned with recording the theme of *anti*-urbanism in American writing and thinking, it would be absurd to argue that *every* great writer or thinker in the American pantheon was hostile to urban life. The fact is that at the end of the nineteenth century there emerged a tendency to view the American city in a more friendly manner. By contrast to his brother Henry, William James had very little desire to escape from the American city into the past. His philosophy was one of hope, of optimism, of possibility—indeed, a little bit too much so—and it was this that allowed him to view the urbanization of America in a way that might encourage Americans to do something about urban problems. Unlike Henry, he did not adore the great cities of Western Europe. For ten days after his arrival in Florence in 1875 he "was so disgusted with the swarming and reeking blackness of the streets and the age of everything, that enjoyment took place under protest."[20] As for London, during his visit of 1889 he wrote his sister that he was "thoroughly sated" with it, and "never cared to see its yellow-brownness and stale spaciousness again."[21]

William James loved the country but his love of nature was tempered by a fondness for sociability, and therefore he was unable to subscribe either to Thoreau's primitivism or to the ultracivilized sentiments of his brother. With Emerson he looked to the future, but unlike Emerson he did not think that the future excluded the possibility of a decent life in the cities of America. Many of William James's reactions to the buzzing confusion of New York of 1880 and 1900 had been unfavorable because of "the clangor, disorder and permanent earthquake conditions" which he experienced on his customary daylong visits. But in 1907 he spent a longer time there and, as he says, "caught the pulse of the machine, took up the rhythm, and vibrated *mit*, and found it simply magnificent."[22] He spoke of it as an "*entirely* new New York, in soul as well as in body, from the old one, which looks like a village in retrospect. The courage, the heaven-scaling audacity of it all, and the *lightness* withal, as if there were nothing that was not easy, and the great pulses and bounds of progress, so many in directions all simultaneous that the coordination is indefinitely future, give a drumming background of life that I have never felt before. I'm sure that once *in* that movement, and at home, all other places would seem insipid."[23] This was written to his brother, of all people, after the appearance of the latter's *The American Scene*, but William had evidently read the manuscript, for he says: "I observe that your book—'The American Scene'—dead H., is just out. I must get it and devour again the chapters relative to New York." William would not have liked them upon rereading them, and one can imagine how Henry must have winced when William exclaimed, "I'm surprised at you, Henry, not having been more enthusiastic, but perhaps the superbly powerful subway was not opened when you were there!"[24]

William James, like Walt Whitman, saw virtue and promise

in the American city. Both William James and Whitman not only accept the city as an inescapable part of America, but they *enjoy* it, as Jefferson most certainly did not. The year of William James's discovery of what he called "the new New York" was 1907, when he delivered his most famous set of lectures, entitled *Pragmatism,* at Columbia. James thought his philosophy would mediate between the views of those whom he called "tenderfoot Bostonians" and those he labeled "Rocky Mountain toughs" in philosophy. It is not too fanciful to suppose that James identified the great future city, along with his pragmatic philosophy, as a blend of, a compromise between, the insipidity of Boston and the craggy brutality of the Rockies. A livable city on earth, one is tempted to say, is the social counterpart of James's pragmatism, and therefore he is one of the first great American writers to associate himself with the effort to accept what is good and to root out what is bad in the American city. He does not escape to the country with Emerson and Thoreau, or to the past with his brother and Henry Adams. He revives the wisdom of the older Jefferson after a century of Transcendentalism, Brook-farming, and expatriation, and adds to it a love of the city. In doing so he becomes the herald of a pragmatic phase in urban thinking.

But this pragmatic phase, in which the city was joyfully described by Frederic C. Howe in 1905 as "The Hope of Democracy," did not last very long. Indeed, Howe's book contained within itself the classical argument for the central city's impending destruction. "The open fields about the city are inviting occupancy," Howe said, "and there the homes of the future will surely be. The city proper will not remain the permanent home of the people. Population must be dispersed. The great cities of Australia are spread out into the suburbs in a splendid way. For miles about are broad roads, with small houses, gardens, and an opportunity for touch with the freer, sweeter life which the country offers."[25] Howe calls the city the hope of democracy, but he is, it would appear, a suburban booster rather than a city-lover. He shares the basic inability of greater American intellectuals to go all out in their admiration for the modern American city.

A more striking illustration of the same thing may be found in the writings of John Dewey, the disciple of William James, who sympathized with so much of James's interest in the American city. In his earlier writing Dewey expressed a typically progressive interest in the city. This was part of the political liberalism of the period, with its interest in urban planning, social work, socialism, the single tax, and muckraking. The city was not regarded as a perfect form of life, but it was seen as having promise. And, to the extent to which it showed promise, it became the concern of all sorts of people who could criticize it in a constructive spirit quite different from that which dominated the work of militant anti-urbanists from Jefferson to Henry James. For a variety of reasons Chicago became the most conspicuous locale of this new way of looking at the city. It was the home of a great university, which had opened its doors in the 'nineties and which became a center of urban sociology and, it might be said, of urban philosophy. One can understand, therefore, why William James looked to Dewey and other Chicago intellectuals as his friends, and why they regarded him as their spiritual leader. For Chicago at the turn of the century was the home of James's pupil, Robert Park, his worshipper, Jane Addams, and his disciple, John Dewey.

As early as 1899 Dewey was urging that the congregation of men into cities was one of the most conspicuous features of the modern world and that no theory of education could possibly disregard the fact of urbanization. Indeed, *the* problem of education, as Dewey saw it in his *School and Society*, was how to adjust the child to life in the city. The earlier kind of rural environment, in which he had been raised as a boy in Vermont, had its virtues, he admitted. It encouraged habits of personal orderliness, industry, and responsibility; it led to a firsthand acquaintance with nature. But, Dewey said in 1899, "it was useless to bemoan the departure of the good old days . . . if we expect merely by bemoaning and by exhortation to bring them back."[26] The problem, as Dewey saw it, was that of retaining some advantages of the older mode of life while training the child to cope with the new urban world. The school, therefore, was to be a miniature urban community, a microcosmic duplication of macrocosmic Chicago, much as Hull House was in Jane Addams' eyes. The essence of society, said Dewey—and in this he was joined by Robert Park and other sociologists—was communication—and therefore the school was to encourage and develop this peculiarly social phenomenon, this salient feature of the urban age. Dewey's progressivism in educational theory was defined by his broad conception of communication, his idea that it takes place while children are building blocks, dancing, and cooking, as well as on the more formal level of asserting propositions.

Later, however, a new and more critical attitude toward the city began to enter Dewey's writing. In *The Public and Its Problems* (1927) he concluded that steam and electricity, the very forces that had created modern society, that had provided it with the means of transportation and communication making urban concentration possible, were creating a situation in which communication at its most human level was being destroyed. The very forces which brought Bangkok and Chicago closer to each other and which brought people from isolated farms to urban centers had diminished the possibility of "face-to-face" relationships. The primary group, in the phrase of the sociologist, Charles Horton Cooley, was disappearing rapidly. And while Dewey did not use our current jargon, he said, in effect, that modern society was becoming a lonely crowd of organization men.

Dewey warned: "Unless local communal life can be restored, the public cannot adequately resolve its most urgent problem: to find and identify itself."[27] But the local communal unit of which Dewey spoke now was not the enormous city as it was coming to be known in the twentieth century. It was more like the University Elementary School at the University of Chicago, or Hull House. "Democracy must begin at home," Dewey said, "and its home is the neighborly community."[28] As a result, a curious reversal takes place in Dewey's thinking. Instead of taking the city as the model *for* the progressive school, he almost speaks as though the urban community should be modeled *on* the progressive school. Jefferson wrote at the end of his life: "As Cato concluded every speech with the words, 'Carthago delenda est,' so do I every opinion with the injunction, 'Divide the counties into wards.' " At the end of his life Dewey seemed to conclude every speech with the words, "Divide the cities into settlement houses."

It is ironic to find the most influential philosopher of the urban age in America reverting to the localism of Jefferson, but no more ironic than the anti-urbanism of Louis Sullivan and Frank Lloyd Wright, our most distinctive architects. For functionalism, like pragmatism, is one of a complex of American ideas that could not exist in a nonurban society, and yet its greatest spokesmen seem to hate the American city. Sullivan's *Autobiography* records his distaste for Boston in his childhood, and in his *Kindergarten Chats* he fulminates against New York and Chicago. "Lieber Meister," as Wright called Sullivan, bequeathed this hostility to his disciple, and the disciple, as everyone knows, added his own powerful spice to the brew of anti-urbanism. John Dewey may have reverted to Jefferson's localism, but Wright was a little more partial to Emerson. Not only are there copious references to Emerson in Wright's books, but he adds as a red-printed appendix to *The Living City* a long excerpt from Emerson's essay, "Farming," which concludes with a typical Transcendentalist warning: "Cities force growth and make men talkative and entertaining, but they make them artificial." And so the great American architect of the twentieth century went back spiritually to Concord, while the great American philosopher retreated to Monticello.

One moral of this tale is that city-loving urban reformers will not find much boosting or sentimental admiration of city life in the writings of those who have been canonized in our national literature and philosophy. A brief flurry of pro-urban sentiment in the late nineteenth and early twentieth century under the encouraging eye of Walt Whitman and William James was swiftly buried by the exploding megalopolis, but after it our most sensitive and gifted intellectuals went on criticizing the American city. Readers who may feel that this story is based on an excessively narrow selection of writers and thinkers should remember that other readers will find in these pages the names of our greatest political thinker, our greatest essayist, our greatest philosopher, our greatest theorist of education, our greatest novelist, our greatest autobiographer, and our greatest architect, all of them throwing up their hands about the most distinctive and most pressing features of our national life. If *their* views should not be typical of the nation's view on this topic, that in itself would be a fact that is worth recording and pondering. Moreover, it is impossible to produce a list of *pro*-urban American thinkers who remotely approach this collection in distinction and intellectual influence.

In spite of the anti-urbanism of our literary and philosophical tradition, the city planner would make a grave mistake if he were to dismiss that tradition, if he were to treat it as a point of view from which nothing could be learned, if he were to forget it and disregard it. Those who must live in today's American city or who like to live in it can profit by taking seriously the urban criticism of our great writers, for it was deep and many-sided. It was not only esthetic but also moral in character. Henry James spoke most persuasively for those who saw the city as a scene of chaos as it presented itself to "the painter's eye." It lacked order, structure, history, and dignity in 1907, and God knows that these virtues have not been miraculously supplied in the age of urban sprawl and suburban slums. But the city, as Robert Park said, is a state of mind as well as an esthetic object, and the profoundest critics of the American city have found other faults with it.

When Jefferson warned of the dangers of what he called the city mob, when Emerson complained of the city's artificiality and conventionalism, when John Dewey lamented the decline of neighborliness, all of them thought of the city as a place in which certain basic human values were being subverted, values which are cherishable today as they were in the eighteenth century of Jefferson, the nineteenth century of Emerson, and the twentieth century of Dewey. And what are these values? Jefferson's worry about the mobs of the city arose from doubt about the American city's capacity to educate its inhabitants in a way that would preserve and extend the democratic process. And when Emerson worried about the growth of artificiality and conventionalism in the city, he was thinking, as were his contemporaries, Kierkegaard and John Stuart Mill, about the increase in conformity, about the decline of individuality which was proportional to the increase of urbanization in America. Dewey's main concern was with the improvement of human communication within the city; and by communication he did not mean the exchange of information alone. He valued the capacity to share feelings and experiences, the capacity to discuss with, to learn from and intelligently persuade others, and to *live* with them in the profoundest sense.

Who can deny in 1961, then, that the great problem of the American city is to demonstrate at least three things: first, that it can solve the problem of education for the millions of people who are entering its gates, that it can absorb the Puerto Rican, as it has other immigrant groups, into the democratic process; second, that it can foster individuality, the capacity and the right of the human being to develop into a rounded personality who is concerned with more than merely commercial values; and third, that it can be more than a vast prison of unconnected cells in which people of different occupations, color, class, or creed fail to understand one another on the basic human issues of social life, let alone agree with one another?

The moral message of the intellectual critic of the city today is not fundamentally different from what it was in the age of Jefferson, Emerson, and Dewey. For today's serious thinker must also build upon a respect for the fundamental values of education, individuality, and easy communication among men. But, unlike his predecessors, he cannot deceive himself about the *place* in which those values must be realized today. The wilderness, the isolated farm, the plantation, the self-contained New England town, the detached neighborhood are things of the past. All the world's a city now and there is no escaping urbanization, not even in outer space.

REFERENCES

1. The theme of this essay is being developed more fully in a larger work. Much of the research and writing has been done under the auspices of the Twentieth Century Fund's Study of Megalopolis, directed by Jean Gottmann, and of the Joint Center for Urban Studies of the Massachusetts Institute of Technology and Harvard University.

2. Perry Miller (editor), *Consciousness in Concord* (Boston: Houghton Mifflin, 1958), p. 46.

3. Henry James, *Hawthorne* (New York: Harper, 1880), p. 80.

4. Harry Levin, *The Power of Blackness* (New York: Knopf, 1958), p. 234.

5. Alexis de Tocqueville, *Democracy in America* (New York: Knopf, 1945), vol. I, p. 289, note.

6. *Ibid.*

7. Arthur M. Schlesinger, *Paths to the Present* (New York: Macmillan, 1949), pp. 223-225.

8. Henry Adams, *The Education of Henry Adams* (Boston: Houghton Mifflin, 1918), pp. 7-8.

9. *Ibid.*, p. 238.

10. Henry James, *The American Scene* (reprint, New York: Scribner's, 1946), p. 77.

11. *Ibid.*, p. 92.

12. *Ibid.*, p. 84.

13. *Ibid.*, p. 279.

14. *Ibid.*, pp. 275, 280.

15. *Ibid.*, p. 85.

16. *Ibid.*, p. 86.

17. *Ibid.*

18. *Ibid.*, p. 115.

19. F. O. Mathiessen, Introduction to *The American Novels and Stories of Henry James* (New York: Knopf, 1947), p. x.

20. Ralph Barton Perry, *The Thought and Character of William James* (Boston, 1935), vol. I, p. 351.

21. *Ibid.*, p. 412.

22. Henry James (editor), *The Letters of William James* (Boston: Atlantic Monthly Press, 1920), vol. II, p. 264.

23. *Ibid.*

24. *Ibid.*

25. Frederic C. Howe, *The City: The Hope of Democracy* (New York, 1905), p. 204.
26. John Dewey, *The School and Society* (Chicago: University of Chicago Press, 1899), p. 9.
27. Dewey, *The Public and Its Problems* (reprint edn., Chicago, 1946), p. 216.
28. *Ibid.*, p. 213.

12. *Utopian Traditions and the Planning of Cities*

MARTIN MEYERSON

In 1516 Sir Thomas More published *Utopia,* thus kindling for the Renaissance as well as for our own times a literary tradition describing an ideal future society and by implication criticizing the society already in existence. A half-century earlier, two Italian architects, Leone Battista Alberti and Filareti (the pseudonym of Antonio Averlino), kindled a parallel utopian tradition of designing the ideal city. Alberti's proposals and Filareti's Sforzinda (a scheme for such a city, dedicated to Francesco Sforza), like More's Utopia, initiated other efforts to depict a desirable pattern for future living—but without saying how to achieve it. Curiously, these two traditions did not influence each other but developed apart. The literary utopias constructed a desirable future in terms of altered social organizations and institutions. The design utopias portrayed a desirable future in terms of altered artifacts and the organization of space.

C. P. Snow has censured the division of contemporary intellectual life into two separate cultures, that of the humanists and that of the natural scientists. Yet that division is no more marked than is the intellectual division between verbal and visual culture. The verbal or social utopias, if they have dealt at all with elements of physical environment, have done so but superficially: the forms and interrelations of housing, workshops, facilities for education and recreation, and the distri-

bution of open land, have followed, as afterthoughts, alterations in property, in family, in political and other institutions.
Conversely, the utopias of visual design have ignored class
structure, the economic base, and the process of government
in the desirable future they present.

Despite their mutual isolation, these two traditions have
some remarkable similarities. Most of the creators of social
utopias believe that man will be happier, more productive, or
more religious—or "better," according to some moral criterion—
if the institutions of society are altered. Most of the creators of
the physical utopias imply that men will be healthier, more
orderly, more satisfied, more inspired by beauty—better in
some other way, if the physical environment is appropriately
arranged. In both cases, utopia has a strong environmental and
moralistic cast: if men are only placed within a proper setting
(whether social or physical), they will behave as the creators
of utopia believe they should behave.

More importantly, the two traditions have another trait in
common—caricature. Man has neither the wisdom, nor the
knowledge, nor the skills in communication to present a cosmic
portrayal of a total future, let alone a total desirable future,
even though some utopias, both social and physical, presume
to such a totality. Not only do the social utopias evade the
physical environment, just as the physical kind of utopia
evades social organization, but even in their own spheres the
limitations of human understanding result in simplifications
and therefore in exaggerations which often have a ludicrous
aspect. The creator of utopia selects a few principles on which
his desirable future society pivots; these may refer to certain
social institutions or to certain conditions in the physical environment. Indeed, utopia can do no more than this. The
anthropologist who tries to study a whole culture achieves
insights only into segments of that culture; the psychologist
does not comprehend the whole personality, but only facets of
it. The utopian creator can only be selective and arbitrary in
his constructs. While the analysis of the social scientist is also

a partial one, his product, if he is capable, is not a caricature; he deals with the present, not the imagined future, and he describes rather than prescribes. The arbitrary, simplified view (or caricature) that has dominated utopias, on the other hand, has often left critics unsure as to whether their creators intended a parody or not.

Since utopias usually result in caricature, intellectuals have rarely been drawn to producing them. The large-scale, internally consistent panoramas of a desirable future often seem too constrained to attract them; or if they are activists, they dismiss utopias as impractical—the absence of any suggested means of achieving the ends makes the effort ridiculous. Moreover, since the Enlightenment, the intellectual's belief in rational progress has gradually eroded: the sophisticate is cynical rather than hopeful for man's prospects. Very rarely has a first-rate mind invented a utopia. When intellectuals, particularly those of the twentieth century, have chosen to caricature the world, they have constructed anti-utopias, panoramas their creators consider as undesirable and therefore as warnings. Perhaps the nature of caricature is best exploited when it is satiric rather than benign. As Margaret Mead says, Hell is always more vivid—and convincing—than Heaven.[1]

Certainly, the sharpest intellectual contributions have been critical even when recommendatory, nor have they been attempts to portray the proposed future. Karl Marx tried systematically to demolish bourgeois society and to demonstrate the inevitable downfall of capitalism, but he said almost nothing about the future conditions of society under his brand of socialism. He (and Engels), scorning other socialists as "utopian," dismissed their proposals for the good society as unrealistic, but he offered no substitute. Socialism, it was thought, would develop its own logic, its own rules and dialectic of change. Apart from some vague predictions that the potentialities of man's creativity would be freed when socialism is achieved, Marx did not indicate what pattern of life would emerge. In a like sense, Freud systematically attacked the prevailing views of human personality and detailed a process by which man might rid himself of his psychic impediments, but he did not indicate what the successfully analyzed personality would be like, or what the form of a society of such personalities would be like.

The greatest contributions of such minds came through their analyses rather than through the development of normative imagery. They were committed to change; their subtle and complicated minds rebutted the static in the human condition. They were not inclined (or were unable) to detail the end products of the changes they desired. Yet the power of their critical and analytical systems revolutionized men's ways of thinking and behaving.

David Riesman in his brilliant essay on utopias calls for a revival of utopian thinking as an intellectual challenge, precisely because it takes more courage to deal with what might be than with what is, and because it is more difficult to pose great alternatives than to choose among lesser evils.[2] Without genuinely revolutionary changes in society, changes that demand substantial sacrifice, substantial gains in human well-being will not be made; to aim at lesser goals, he believes, may make for a real waste of human talents, since the goal least likely to be achieved is the maintenance of the *status quo.*

It is not the motivational value of utopia, however, that I am affirming so much as its potential contribution to planning—specifically, to the planning of cities. The attributes of the utopian caricature, if they are recognized as caricature, can be extremely useful in posing potentially desirable ends and then in testing these ends with a logical model. Would such ends, if carried out consistently, result in a desirable state of affairs or not? Utopia specifies a desirable future state without detailing the means of achieving it. City planning is charged with specifying a desirable future state and also the means of attaining it.

City planning as a vocation has become widely accepted in the last few decades, particularly in English-speaking countries. The literature of city planning claims as one of its purposes and competencies the preparation of long-range, comprehensive plans for communities. In practice, however, city planning has either ignored the means (while still not proposing fundamental changes) or it has concentrated on the efficacy of means to the exclusion of ends.

As city planning clarifies its theory and sharpens its methodology, it will be faced with the choice of relinquishing the utopian elements now residual in its ideology or of capitalizing on them. I suggest that city planners ought to recognize the value of utopian formulations in the depicting of the community as it might be seen through alternative normative lenses.

City planning, in portraying a future state of affairs, tries to link economic and social policy with physical design to solve such urban problems as housing and transportation. The two separate traditions of utopia, that of artifact and that of institutions, can simultaneously be drawn upon for this objective. By developing alternative utopias of the community, both in physical or material terms and in social and economic terms, city planning would not remove the element of caricature. Instead, it would give that element meaning, since caricature would sharpen the scrutiny of the consequences of following alternative sets of ends and means.

It is the utopian process—the sketching out of the implications of altering certain fundamental features of society and environment—that should be emulated, rather than the utopian product. Indeed, since utopias are so diverse in their portrayals of the good life (or, in the case of the anti-utopia, the evil life), as Raymond Ruyer observes, the process of formulation is the main feature they have in common.[3]

The social utopias of the past have sought many goals— political, social, religious freedom, sexual freedom, economic freedom, freedom of movement, and freedom from industrialization. They have suggested some fundamental changes in society to obtain these various goals. Freedom from want is a

recurrent theme, especially in the utopias of early capitalism
and industrialism. While the prototype utopias, such as Plato's
Republic, were most of all concerned with moral values, the
later ones often combined these with economic welfare. The
utopias of the last few hundred years have often postulated
material abundance as a major theme.

Each of the classic literary utopias became a caricature
when it dealt with moral values and material abundance together. Almost all these caricatures were based on rationality,
on the rational control of men's actions, on the participation
of all in the work of the society, and on the manipulation of
institutions.

Sir Thomas More, who coined the word "utopia," postulated
an ascetic abundance, that is, an abundance of basic goods
without luxury or ornament. Despite his Catholicism, his good
society anticipated some of the features of the Protestant ethic,
which later provided an ideology to reinforce the development of the civilization of industrial capitalism. This ideology
emphasized work, thrift, self-restraint, and the voluntary ful-
fillment of one's duty. In More's Utopia the theme of material
abundance was linked to the themes of work and participation.
Each individual in Utopia had to participate actively in the
affairs of the society and do his part of the work to achieve the
benefits of the society. This triple achievement of abundance,
participation, and work was to be brought about by elaborate
sets of rigid social controls, social rewards, and punishments.

By rotating city and country living, men would acquire
knowledge and working skills in both areas. Syphogrants, or
magistrates, each elected to supervise thirty families, were responsible for seeing that all worked at their tasks. Deviations
from work or from other requirements of the community were
punished by sanctions, such as slavery.

Even in their leisure time, "all men live in full view, so that
all are obliged . . . to employ themselves well in their spare
hours." More's society simplified this obligation by forbidding
all alehouses, taverns, gambling, and other vices, and by frown-

ing on such activities as hunting. Intellectual pleasures were encouraged by the example of Utopia's selected group of scholars and by the whole educational system, which taught that spare hours should be spent in reading or attending lectures. Thus the society achieved a level of abundance for which all worked and in which all participated. The level of abundance was maintained in part because the population was to be stationary. More, like Malthus after him, had but limited faith in the potentialities of increasing labor productivity and he feared overpopulation. If there should be an excess of people in Utopia, room for expansion would be found on an adjacent continent.

America, which became the outlet for Europe's expanding population, came to be regarded as a utopian setting. In a Rousseau-like fashion, some utopian thinkers subsequent to More conceived of colonial American society as resembling the simple, ascetic and "happy" life of the Indians rather than the corrupt and sophisticated life of the Europeans. Books such as *The Kingdom of Paradise*[4] assumed that the settlers in America became Indianized, and some writers even described the American Indian as the successor of the Greeks, and portrayed him wearing Greek dress.

Furthermore, there were two hundred or more utopias put into actual practice in America, but these communities (such as Owen's New Harmony, Oneida, the so-called Love Colony, and Brook Farm, the colony of the intellectuals) failed. Most of them failed, not through economic disaster, but through economic abundance. Almost all stressed group solidarity, rigidly defined social roles, hard work, participation—attitudes and functions which were indispensable to the battle against adversity but which dissipated when economic prosperity arrived.

New Harmony, Indiana, founded in 1824 by Robert Owen, the English industrialist, represented an applied effort to achieve a set of goals, some of which he described in his book, *A New View of Society*. In its rather cryptic last paragraph, he indicated that his scheme as written was only a compromise within the existing system of industrialization, against whose brutality he revolted. Owen believed that industry, if it were properly organized, would require but little labor and that it would at the same time provide abundance. He proposed, as did More, a simple physical structure of the community: most of its features would be collective—community dining halls, lecture halls, work places, and even sleeping quarters for the children. Owen, like More, stressed work, education, and participation. He expected that at New Harmony the ideals expressed in its constitution would be self-evident and therefore enforced by individuals and the group alike. These ideals included an equality of duties, community of property, and "cooperative union in the business and amusements of life."

These ideals were not realized at New Harmony. Within three years the community failed, but without having achieved the economic abundance that proved to be the nemesis of the other applied American utopias. There were ample facilities for employment for its eight hundred recruits, but there were no effective social controls to ensure conformity among the various kinds of personalities the community attracted. Owen had believed that the necessary behavioral responses would come spontaneously. He imported a "Boatload of Knowledge," a group of scholars to lead the intellectual life of the community. He proclaimed equality, with an attack on private property, in "A Declaration of Mental Independence," which he believed would become as significant as the Declaration of Independence. Nevertheless, without built-in sanctions and rewards, the colonists lacked motives for performing as he anticipated. Lewis Mumford declares that a contributing cause of failure was the character of Owen himself, "whose bumptiousness, arrogance, and conceit were bound to provoke reactions in other people which would have defeated the plans of Omnipotence itself."[5]

More wrote at a time when capitalism was emerging, Owen, at a time when the early industrial revolution was showing both some of its promise and some of its brutalizing effects. In America, some of these effects became most apparent near the end of the nineteenth century, and probably as a result, in the 1890's more utopian books were published in America than at any other time anywhere. Edward Bellamy's novel, *Looking Backward* (1888) heralded this outburst. It sold over a million copies in America alone—the largest seller, and to John Dewey the most influential, since *Uncle Tom's Cabin*. It inspired many similar works and prompted the formation of a large group of nationalist clubs organized to carry out Bellamy's vision.

Almost all the American literary utopias of the 'nineties conceived of the problems of society as economic. Almost all assumed that technicians could provide for society. Almost all assumed that human want could be eradicated through technological innovation and economic organization. The idea of conformity to the group pattern dominated this literature. One of Bellamy's protagonists described the compulsory labor service as being so natural and reasonable that it was no longer considered compulsory and commented, "Our entire social order is so wholly based upon and deduced from it that if it were conceivable that a man could escape from it, he would be left with no possible way to provide for his existence. He would have excluded himself from the world, cut himself off from his kind, in a word, committed suicide."

Bellamy's world was rational, orderly, friendly, technologically advanced (he foresaw the radio and other inventions), and offered material abundance not only to provide for basic needs but also for leisure. His world, too, was a static and rigid one. Bellamy, like Owen and More, saw in the utopian ideal a possibility for abundance that could be achieved only through a participation in the society and through work. To ensure participation in work, and thus abundance, strong social sanctions had to be established and conforming types of personality projected as suitable for the members of utopia. Only Charles Fourier, who recognized that

work could be disagreeable and rewarded disagreeable work
with the highest pay, conceived of a utopia in which minority
tastes and behavior could be satisfied and a diversity of interests encouraged. Yet Fourier failed to envisage the potentialities of industrialization.

Utopias founded on a faith in mechanization and constructed
at a time when the possibilities of industrialization were just
unfolding did not encompass a pluralistic, permissive society.
For achieving abundance through technology, they depended
on the solidarity of a kind of folk society, a solidarity that may
have been a realistic appraisal of the pressures necessary to
shift nonindustrial workers into industrial occupations. The
anti-utopians, such as William Graham Sumner in his "Cooperative Commonwealth," Aldous Huxley in *Brave New
World*, and George Orwell in *1984*, satirize the rigidity, the
totalitarian smugness and joyless security of utopia. Indeed,
if utopias can be traced as far back as Plato's conception of the
ideal state, then anti-utopias are at least as old as Aristophanes'
The Birds, and their central theme is man's lack of freedom
within a supposedly good society.

Certainly, the classical social utopias justify the charge that
they present end products, not processes. They envisage no
future change, they do not provide for it, they give no indication that society does evolve. Although in utopian literature
man is supposed to choose the good life willingly when he is
exposed to its advantages, his natural bent is not trusted, and
therefore his behavior is proscribed. A person in More's Utopia,
for example, was under constant observation by his neighbors
and the magistrates, not only during his work hours but also
in his leisure time, so that he should spend it correctly. Slavery
was the punishment for two unauthorized journeys from one's
city, and death, for any private political discussion. In Bellamy's new society, the inspectorate was alert in checking
aberrations from the standards. In these utopias there is security—mainly the security of material well-being. What is
sacrificed is the development of a wide spectrum of diversified

personalities and the opportunity to express them. The complacency, the denial of change, and the imposition of a set of rigid sanctions and ideals cannot help but produce stereotyped personalities. The stereotyped citizen of utopia is as smug and complacent as the society that produces him.

W. S. Gilbert and Arthur Sullivan parody utopian complacency in their comic opera, *Utopia Limited, or the Flowers of Progress,* in which Utopia is converted by England, through a Utopian princess who had attended a British finishing school. When a Utopian citizen asks, "Then in a few months, Utopia may . . . be completely Anglicized?" the reply is, "Absolutely and without a doubt." At this a Utopian maiden complains, "We are very well as we are. Life without a care—every want supplied. . . . What have we to gain by the great change that is in store for us?" Her friend answers, "What have we to gain? English institutions, English tastes, and oh, English fashions." Near the end of the play, with the conversion accomplished, the chorus sings,

> In short, this happy country has been Anglicized completely!
> It really is surprising
> What a thorough Anglicizing
> We have brought about—Utopia's quite another land;
> In her enterprising movements,
> She is England—with improvements,
> Which we dutifully offer to our mother-land.

> *King:* Our city we have beautified—we've done it willy-nilly—
> And all that isn't Belgrave Square is Strand and Piccadilly.

The complacency, rigidity, and lack of opportunity for deviant behavior that characterized the utopias of the emerging industrial civilization persisted in those of the twentieth century. In its early years the literary and social utopia went into eclipse, but the physical or design utopia of the ideal city, through the work of Frank Lloyd Wright and Le Corbusier, achieved relative prominence. Each of these architects produced a twentieth-century utopia amid flourishing technical advances and an urbanized society. Half a century earlier, James Silk Buckingham, an English manufacturer, had called for a trust-like organization to construct a new town, to be called Victoria, as a physical utopia with the latest technical improvements. Wright and Le Corbusier, alarmed yet fascinated by industrial civilization, concluded that a new physical setting, such as they could create on the drawing board, was the right means of remaking industrial civilization.

One of the principles on which Le Corbusier based his ideal city was, "A city made for speed is made for success." The railroad station stood at the center of the city, like the hub of a wheel, linked to subways, buses, and other transportation facilities, and to the airfield by helicopter. His scheme for Paris (or any large city) was devised shortly after World War I. Near the center stood twenty-four skyscrapers, each sixty stories high; these great complexes served the commercial needs of the community; in the surrounding parks were luxurious restaurants, theatres, and shops. Most people lived in well-spaced, high, elevator apartment buildings with private hanging gardens for each unit, although a few lived in colonies of individual houses. The streets were on three levels so as to provide for different types of vehicles traveling at different speeds. The high degree of density concentrated people efficiently into small areas, thus freeing large areas for agriculture, recreation, and the contemplation of nature. Such a geometrically spaced urban development permitted many services, cultural and other, that require a concentrated consumer population and an adequate transportation system. Le Corbusier's conception of the city as a machine, or a complex of machines, for daily living also conferred on all men the right to light, greenery, spaciousness, silence, privacy, and beauty—rights otherwise enjoyed only by the peasantry and the privileged.

Whereas Le Corbusier postulated a concentrated urban society, Wright's idea was to disperse people and their activities. He built a large-scale model called Broadacre City and wrote several books setting forth his ideal society of Usonia (the term was borrowed from Butler's *Erewhon*). In Usonia the citizens were to live each on an acre or so of ground on which they could grow vegetables, and for occasional employment they were to commute to a factory some miles away. There were to be small institutions such as universities and museums proportionate in size to the small homesteads, all connected by automotive transportation. Wright believed that the fusion of town and country would be accomplished by the diffusion of city functions throughout the land. Whereas Marx and Engels wanted to eliminate what they called the "idiocy of country life" by revising the differentiation between town and country, Wright aimed at eliminating what he regarded as the idiocy of city life.

Although neither Wright nor Le Corbusier dealt with the economic, social, or political aspects of their new societies, it is obvious that each made very different use of resources, and each had a different conception of the organization of social institutions, as well as of the behavioral and living patterns best suited to a people. They both assumed that if men are captivated by the prospect of a reorganized physical environment, they will create the institutions to obtain it. Their faith in the possibility of designing an urban utopia of the physical environment has spread to such mass media as the Sunday supplement, science fiction, and advertising copy.

Today any technological innovation appears feasible, even a reorganization of the total environment of the earth, and schemes for diverting the Gulf Stream so as to warm Greenland, melt the polar ice caps, and provide rich fish-farming areas are discussed in the responsible press. Any amount of consumption seems possible: an increase in comfort and esthetic satisfaction, as well as the abolition of drudgery, are promised. The folklore of modern utopia provides many a glimpse of effortless abundance and a life of ease. In popular culture confidence in the future as a bigger and better present is perceptible everywhere.[6] In his 1952 campaign, Adlai Stevenson stated, "I do say to you soberly and sincerely that on the evidence of science, of technology, and of our own common sense, the United States at mid-century stands on the threshold of abundance for all, so great as to exceed the happiest dream of the pioneers who opened the vast Western country. Unless we allow ourselves to be held back by fear, we shall in God's good time realize the golden promise of our future."[7]

When the automatic factory and office are commoner, the major problem will perhaps be, not motivation for work, but motivation for leisure pursuits. How are the former workers to be kept innocuously occupied? When productivity continues rising, it is not the satisfaction of wants but the creation of new wants that is challenging. Obviously, the old utopias are obsolete; the dream of material abundance is already a popular expectation and a component of the modern utopia.

When the great social utopias were created, at least two attitudes were prevalent: dissatisfaction with present conditions; and hope, even confidence, of change through man's mastery of his environment. If people feel complacent, they will not be motivated to change. If, on the other hand, they feel powerless and estranged, they will lack the courage and energy to venture into the unknown. Many contemporary observers have pointed to a combination of affluence and apathy that induces a complacency both in Americans and Western Europeans. On the one hand, high levels of employment and a rising standard of living inhibit any popular urge toward change. On the other hand, problems that are too complex and too removed from individual competence inhibit a sense of effective action. Thus the contemporary utopian folklore is in a sense reinforced by the complacency resulting from the material affluence that has spread throughout our middle class as well as through many groups of industrial workers and by the feeling of impotence deriving from the alienation of the citizen from the making of important decisions. By reinforcing the theme of automatic abundance, complacency and the sense of impotence sap the sources of motivation that in the past provided a clientele for social and literary utopias such as

Bellamy's. Furthermore, when the imagery of the redesigned physical environment is taken over from the sophisticated high culture of a Wright or a Le Corbusier by the popular culture of the mass media, the prophetic element of such a utopia is lessened.

At the same time, a radical faith in man's ability to alter his society and his environment in any significant way by planning has increasingly been replaced by a Burkean belief in man's inability to do so. But even a utopian or radical faith does not produce utopias. Oscar Wilde once wrote, "A map of the world that does not include Utopia is not worth even glancing at. . . ." But he did not create a utopia—nor has David Riesman or Martin Buber or Karl Mannheim, other protagonists of utopia.

Since there appears to be little demand for utopia, since no one for a generation has produced social or physical-design utopias of importance, and since utopias are caricatures anyway, this essay amounts to an epitaph—but an epitaph only for the rigid social and physical utopias of the past, for utopia as a product, and not for utopia as a process for clarifying policy, particularly in city planning.

Planning, like utopia, depicts a desirable future state of affairs, but unlike utopia, specifies the means of achieving it. In the Western world, planning, like utopia (and for many of the same reasons), has become suspect. Some of the intellectuals have seen society as too complex, and knowledge as too inadequate, to allow men purposefully to plan their world. But the planning of cities has been exempt from this view. Partly because it does not threaten the equilibrium of economic and political power, partly because cities appear to many to be a glaring failure of decision on the part of the market-place, partly because cities appear to some to be finite enough to comprehend and manage, the planning of cities has become institutionalized as the principal form of public planning in most Western countries.

In so far as city planning deals with the future, it must deal with both innovations in ends or values and innovations in means or courses of action. Utopian formulation is a method for testing innovation in city and other kinds of planning. It is a method that could be used in two ways. First, as I envisage it, it could enable the city planner to set up a series of utopian models, each organized about a different set of principles. Each utopian model could then be logically examined in terms of both the direct and the indirect or side effects of following these principles. Second, after this kind of screening and modifying, the surviving alternative utopian models could be tested by the reactions of civic leaders and the citizenry at large. In 1949 I recommended to public officials in Chicago that a "museum of the future" might highlight the civic possibilities; both leaders and citizens could be encouraged to participate in utopian thinking and thus help resolve policy as to long-term urban development.

This method would share certain characteristics with model-building in a field such as economics. However, most forms of model-building, if therapeutic at all, are adaptive, that is, they are concerned only with incremental changes, and with these changes only as means. Most changes, of course, can be only incremental and can take place only at that level, rather than as ends. But utopian model-building for city policy and planning may even suggest new incremental measures that otherwise would not have been conceived, as well as more drastic paths of desirable action.

Admittedly, these more drastic choices will be in the form of caricatures, but, unlike most utopias, they would be intended as such for the purpose of testing. Furthermore, I have presented a critical review of the utopian tradition largely in the hope that the course just recommended can transcend some of the limitations of past utopias, in particular, by uniting the verbal and the visual, the socio-economic and the physical-environmental traditions. Even if the good social and economic life can be achieved apart from the good physical setting, the setting has a series of human consequences in benefits and costs which should be comprehended.

Another hope is that these models of utopian planning need not be restricted and rigid, as were those of the past. Having achieved a state of technology in which material abundance is no longer in doubt, we can delineate pluralistic urban utopias. We can be more permissive, without leaning on rigid social controls in order to motivate people to work, or on types of personality standardized so as to behave in a prescribed manner, or on the uniform physical patterns of a Wright or a Le Corbusier. This is the age W. W. Rostow characterizes as one of high mass consumption—admittedly, not available to all. Now we can not only permit deviation, we can also encourage it. Utopians now have the task of devising institutions and the material organization of society to free men from the restrictions under which they have previously operated, instead of curtailing men's choices. This may be the time for the post-technological model, in which it is assumed that technical change and material production are so readily available that they cease to be important limiting conditions. If production and technology do wane, utopian formulations can more readily shift from the authoritarian to the permissive view of the human personality, from a kind of statistical concept of central tendency to one of dispersion, satisfying many minority aspirations. But the theme of production and technology itself is one that should undergo exploration in utopian models, for it is a theme that could radically alter the nature of cities, whether emphasized or diminished.

Earlier in this essay I have written that it was the utopian process rather than the utopian specific that should serve as present stimulus and inspiration. If we approach utopias experimentally, tentatively, consciously seeking alternatives, we should be able to avoid the static, complacent rigidity of past social and physical utopias, as the two traditions become blended into a single instrument for the planning of cities.

REFERENCES

1. Margaret Mead, "Towards More Vivid Utopias," *Science*, 1957, *126*: 958.
2. David Riesman, "Some Observations on Community Plans and Utopia," *Yale Law Journal*, December 1947, pp. 173-200.
3. Raymond Ruyer, *L'Utopie et les Utopies* (Paris: Presses Universitaires de France, 1950).
4. For a discussion of this literature, see Michael Kraus, "America and the Utopian Ideal in the Eighteenth Century," *The Mississippi Valley Historical Review*, 1934, *22*: 487-504.
5. Lewis Mumford, *The Story of Utopias* (New York: Boni and Liveright, 1922; Peter Smith reprint, 1941), p. 248.
6. Science fiction has become an exception. In the days when H. G. Wells was proclaiming faith in the progress of technology and science, and even as late as the years immediately following World War II, science fiction seemed devoted to science, and scientists as often as not appeared critical, even fearful, of technology. In the 1950's, science fiction has shifted markedly into the anti-utopia camp, and is filled with satire instead of an enthusiastic endorsement of what is to come.
7. Adlai E. Stevenson, quoted in Clarke A. Chambers, "The Belief in Progress in Twentieth-Century America," *Journal of the History of Ideas*, 1958, *19*: 219.
8. One example of such an enterprising blend is *Communitas: Means of Livelihood and Ways of Life*, by Percival and Paul Goodman, architect and philosopher respectively (Chicago: University of Chicago Press, 1947), a book that has stimulated David Riesman's article (Reference 2 above).

Notes on Contributors

EDWARD C. BANFIELD, born in Bloomfield, Connecticut, in 1916, received his doctoral degree from the University of Chicago and is at present professor of government at Harvard University. Among his publications are: *Politics, Planning and the Public Interest* (with Martin Meyerson), *Government and Housing in Metropolitan Areas* (with Morton Grodzins), and *Political Influence* (forthcoming).

KARL W. DEUTSCH, born in Prague in 1912, is professor of political science at Yale University. Since 1938, when he came to the United States, he has taught in several academic institutions and for a time served as chief of various research sections in Washington. His books include: *The Political Community and the North Atlantic Area, Germany Rejoins the Powers* (with Lewis J. Edinger), and *The Nerves of Government* (forthcoming).

JOHN W. DYCKMAN, born in Chicago in 1922, is professor of city planning at the University of Pennsylvania. His special interests are the economic and social aspects of urbanization and the theory of planning. Among his publications are: *Study of Standards and Requirements for Community Facilities* (with Martin Meyerson and Herbert Gans) and *Capital Requirements for Urban Development and Renewal*.

AARON FLEISHER, born in Brooklyn, is a lecturer in the Department of City and Regional Planning and on the research staff of the Joint Center for Urban Studies of the Massachusetts Institute of Technology and Harvard University. He is currently working on problems of the interaction of patterns of urban density and transportation. His articles have appeared in professional journals in his field.

OSCAR HANDLIN, born in Brooklyn, in 1915, has taught American social history at Harvard University since 1939, and is presently director of the Center to Study the History of Liberty in America. In addition to having edited the Library of American Biography and the *Harvard Guide to American History*, he is the author of many works, including *Boston's Immigrants, The Uprooted* (awarded the Pulitzer Prize), *The American People in the Twentieth Century, Al Smith and His America*, and *Immigration as a Factor in American History*.

GYORGY KEPES, born in Selyp, Hungary, in 1906, is a painter and designer. He worked in Berlin and London on film, stage, and exhibition design (1930-1936). In 1937 he came to the United States to head the Light and Color Department at the Institute of Design in Chicago. Since 1946 he has been professor of visual design at the Massachusetts Institute of Technology. His writings include: *Language of Vision* and *The New Landscape in Art and Science*, and he is the editor of *The Visual Arts Today* (originally published as the Winter 1960 issue of *Dædalus*).

KEVIN LYNCH, born in Chicago in 1918, is a professor of city planning at the Massachusetts Institute of Technology, and is codirector of a ·five-year Rockefeller research project on the perceptual form of the city. He has served as consultant on various planning enterprises, and has recently published *The Image of the City*.

MARTIN MEYERSON, born in New York City in 1922, is Williams professor of city planning and urban research at Harvard University, and also director of the Joint Center for Urban Studies of the Massashusetts Institute of Technology and Harvard. As research director, executive director, and vice-president, he has served ACTION, Inc., a national organization for urban development. His writings include *Politics, Planning and the Public Interest* (with E. C. Banfield).

LLOYD RODWIN, born in New York City in 1919, is chairman of the Faculty Committee of the Joint Center for Urban Studies of the Massachusetts Institute of Technology and Harvard University, and professor of land economics in the Department of City and Regional Planning, MIT. He has served as consultant to the United Nations, the European Productivity Agency of the Organization for European Economic Cooperation, and various government planning projects in Latin America. His publications include *The British New Towns Policy* and *Housing and Economic Progress*.

RAYMOND VERNON, born in New York City in 1913, is professor of international trade and investment at Harvard University, and was director of the New York Metropolitan Region Study. Besides having taught at the Harvard Business School, Princeton University, and Swarthmore College, he has held numerous governmental posts in the fields of economic analysis and policy. His books include: *Anatomy of a Metropolis* and *Metropolis, 1985*.

MORTON WHITE, born in New York City in 1917, is professor of philosophy at Harvard University. He has been a Guggenheim Fellow, a member of the Institute for Advanced Study at Princeton University, and a Fellow of the Center for Advanced Study in the Behavioral Sciences at Stanford, California. His writings include: *The Origin of Dewey's Instrumentalism, Social Thought in America, The Age of Analysis* (editor), *Toward Reunion in Philosophy*, and *Religion, Politics, and the Higher Learning*. LUCIA WHITE, his wife, is collaborating with him on a study of the American intellectual's attitude toward the American city. A graduate of Vassar College and of the New York School for Social Work, she has been active in social work in Boston and New York.